Collected Poems and Other Writings

Robert Menzies

COLLECTED POEMS
AND
OTHER WRITINGS

ROBERT MENZIES

Edited by William Cook, Georgina Downer
and Victoria Hronas

With a Foreword by Dr Stephen McInerney

Jeparit Press

Published in 2025 by Connor Court Publishing Pty Ltd under the Jeparit Press Imprint.

Jeparit Press is an imprint of Connor Court Publishing in conjunction with The Robert Menzies Institute.

Connor Court Publishing Pty Ltd
PO Box 7257
Redland Bay QLD 4165
sales@connorcourt.com
www.connorcourt.com

ISBN: 9781923224452

Cover Design by Maria-Grazia Giordano
Printed in Australia

Several of these poems were discovered in the Menzies Papers held in the National Library of Australia by biographer Troy Bramston, and published for the first time in his book *Robert Menzies: the art of politics* in 2019.

'The truth is that no great book was ever written and no great picture ever painted by the clock or according to civil service rules. These things are done by man, not men. You cannot regiment them. They require opportunity, and sometimes leisure. The artist, if he is to live, must have a buyer; the writer an audience. He finds them among frugal people to whom the margin above bare living means a chance to reach out a little towards that heaven which is just beyond our grasp.'

Robert Menzies, 1942

This compilation was made possible by the generous support of the
Alan and Mary-Louise Archibald Foundation.

Contents

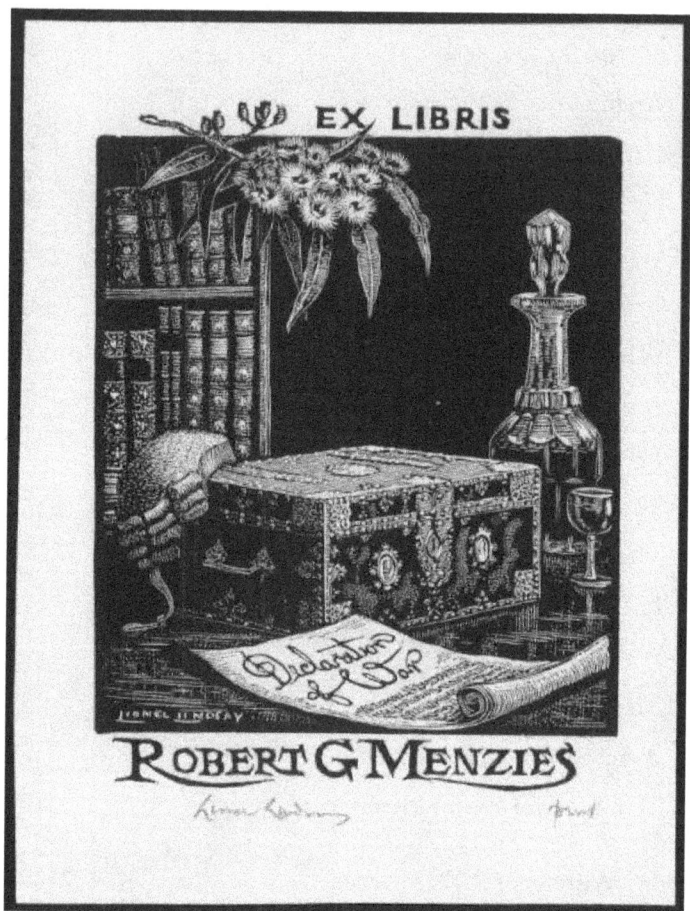

Robert Menzies's personal bookplate, designed by Lionel Lindsay.

Foreword

When I was approached to write the foreword for this volume of Robert Menzies's verse, poetic reflections and university literary articles, I was circumspect. It is not unusual for someone in my position to be approached by undergraduates to read their poetry and offer an opinion and some guidance, but to be approached – as it were – by an undergraduate (albeit through the custodians of his legacy) from more than a hundred years ago, and one moreover who went on to become Australia's longest-serving Prime Minister, is another thing altogether.

Or is it? The Robert Menzies Institute did not ask me to assess whether the works contained herein are of historical interest, which of course they are, but whether they have any literary merit. To arrive at a judgement on that, I decided to evaluate the works by keeping in mind what for the most part they are – the writings of a talented young man undertaking a law degree at a prestigious Australian university, a young man moreover who clearly loves poetry and especially the work of Wordsworth, and who is engaging intelligently with important questions about the relationship between the

English poetic tradition and his own country, even if he is not always conscious that that is what he is doing.

The verse seems at a first glance (and even a second and third glance) to be highly derivative, but this is precisely what one should expect from an undergraduate poet. A better way to understand what's going on here is to recognise that the young poet, who clearly imagines for himself a long career writing poetry, is doing his apprenticeship at the feet of the poets of Palgrave's *Golden Treasury*. As Aristotle said in his *Poetics,* "the instinct for imitation is inherent in human beings from our earliest days... [We] learn our earliest lessons by imitation". Prose writing has always been taught by asking students to copy models of writing produced by others, ideally by the best prose stylists, and the craft of poetry is no different. A young poet usually comes under the spell of a great poet and tries to express his own feelings, or the feelings he would like to feel, in the forms of the master. He learns to write a sonnet by copying out, word for word, his favourite examples, and then learns to supply new thoughts and words to the old forms, perhaps keeping the same rhyming pattern, or even using the same rhyming word at the end of each line but varying the words that lead up to it, and so on. Gradually, progressively, through a series of light touches, false starts, dead ends and new discoveries, by a process of trial and error, he produces something that is recognisably his own and finds in doing so his own voice. When the original work finally arrives, it seems to have come from the skies, from the Muses as it were, but is in fact as much the result of painstaking study as it is of inspiration.

Menzies never really discovered his own voice. Few budding poets do. But what one can say is that the young poet we first encounter in 1912 was serving a very good apprenticeship and may well have gone on to become a good poet had his life not taken the direction it did. He handles traditional forms deftly and often surprises the reader with a carefully chosen phrase, often understated. In "Animi Patrum", for example, which won a prize at Wesley College in 1912, when Menzies was 18, the young poet describes the "bearded pioneers of a new nation" who "set forth in the wilds to find a way". The rest of the poem often resorts to grandiloquence, but "to find a way" is just right and captures the drama of a quest that is by turns both epic and humble. One also notes in this poem a theme that will become something of a preoccupation in Menzies's undergraduate poetry, a concern with a new nation in formation. This is also picked up in his literary articles, mostly written for the University of Melbourne magazine. The emergence of Australia as a small but important nation on the world stage is not simply a political goal but a cultural one. Menzies yearns for the day "when Australian literature will take a very high place among the treasures of all time". That indeed went on to happen. Patrick White won the Nobel Prize for Literature in 1973, and in Judith Wright, A.D. Hope and Les Murray, among half-a-dozen or so other names, Australia produced some of the finest poets of the twentieth century.

Whether Menzies would have approved of the direction Australian literature would take, under the influence of changing currents in England and America, is not really the question. Certainly, he could not have predicted it. When he was working away in Melbourne on his youthful poems and articles in the years of the First World War, poetry in English was on the verge of a transformation. Robert Frost had just published his first two volumes of poetry, *A Boy's Will* and *North of Boston* and had helped Edward Thomas find his poetic voice. Thomas Hardy had just written some of the most poignant elegies in the language, about his late wife, in *Poems 1912-1913*. Over in Paris, T.S. Eliot was writing the poems that would form the basis of his first volume, *Prufrock and Other Observations*. The miraculous body of work produced by Gerard Manley Hopkins in the Victorian period – but hitherto hidden from the public – was about to be released, in 1918, by Robert Bridges, and Wilfred Owen was soon to die, leaving behind him an extraordinary series of poems that utilised traditional forms to shatter traditional patriotic views of warfare. The English poetic tradition that Menzies revered was being remade in ways that would have made it unrecognisable to the young student of the English canon working away in his Melbourne study.

His adult poetry, which is occasional, forgettable and notably inferior to his undergraduate work, seems similarly unaware of the currents of thought, feeling and form that came to dominate British and American poetry in the years between the wars. There is no shame in that. He was a statesman, not a poet. If Menzies did not keep up with new developments in English poetry, he retained nonetheless his love of his first master, Wordsworth, till his dying days, and could recite from memory long passages of *The Prelude*, as he once did (as Judith Brett reports) to the astonished members of an English Chair Committee at the University of Melbourne, during his time as the University's Chancellor.

Of the many Australian poets he read, Menzies preferred Henry Kendall above all others and certainly above the poets of the Bulletin school. He admires in Kendall what he admired in Wordsworth, calling him "a priest of nature" whose lines at their best are "Wordsworthian in their loftiness and their natural religion". Interestingly, Menzies himself is more Wordsworthian in his poetic prose than he is in his verse, and it is also to the poetic reflections that we must look to find him wrestling with the inability of English lines and sentiments to capture the Australian landscape. When he invokes Keats's "mists and mellow fruitfulness" to describe an Australian autumn, he strikes a false note, but elsewhere, when describing the "mountain gums, straight and clean-limbed", one feels he has anticipated something of the sensibility of Robert Gray, Australia's finest landscape poet. Such moments are rare, but one of the pleasures of setting forth through this little volume lies in imagining how many more of them we might have been given, had Menzies become, instead of a lawyer and politician, one of Shelley's "unacknowledged legislators of the world".

The first three sections of this volume, following the foreword contain the verse written by Menzies as a student; his poetic reflections, in prose, on nature; and his reflections on poetry. The final section contains the occasional verse he wrote as a politician and statesman, taken from his papers in the National Library of Australia, Canberra.

Writing in the Melbourne University Magazine in November 1914, the 19-year-old Robert Menzies lamented that students who pride themselves "on having at home an expensively bound copy of their Wordsworth or their Tennyson, should prove their utter hypocrisy and cant by ignoring cheaply the attempts, crude though they be, to express thoughts a little higher than the everyday". More than a hundred years on, the young poet seems to be asking yet again not to be ignored. This volume should ensure he won't be, at least by students of history.

Stephen McInerney

Campion College

May 2024

Robert Menzies circa 1907 at Wesley College, Melbourne.
Source: Menzies Family Collection.

An Editor's Note

Sir Robert Menzies had a grand collection of poetry amongst his small library of over 4,500 books. The poetry takes up a very large portion, which he donated in 1976 to the Bailleu Library at the University of Melbourne, where it is currently housed in the Leigh Scott Room. It should take no one by surprise that he was quite the poet himself.

It would be foolish to lump all of his personal works into a category or reduce them in any way as they cover many subjects from politics to the nature at Mount Macedon. I took great pleasure in the works ranging from the idle ditties about politicians to the serious assessments of the beauty of the Australian countryside. My preference is for his works in his early years at the University of Melbourne and is carrying on like Sebastian from *Brideshead Revisited*.

As a librarian who has catalogued his entire book collection, studied him at length and discovered many unpublished poems, I can say while his poetic works of course do not reach the depths or heights of

Wordsworth, they are certainly insightful for learning how he thought and for what he thought. For this reason, it is important they are published.

Whether one reads the works from the early years or the poems during his political career, I would suggest the critical point is that the unifying theme is that they are all jovial, fun and should be celebrated. Not to do so would show a complete disregard for any modern historian, and indeed entertainer.

William Cook
Robert Menzies Institute
February 2024

The Verse of Menzies in his Student Days

As far back as his student days, Menzies had a passionate interest in poetry. Menzies's poetry can be dated as far back as the age of 10, when he wrote about the local football games in Jeparit, onto Wesley College and throughout Melbourne University. It may come as a surprise that his early poems take on quite a different and rather more serious character to those composed in his later professional life.

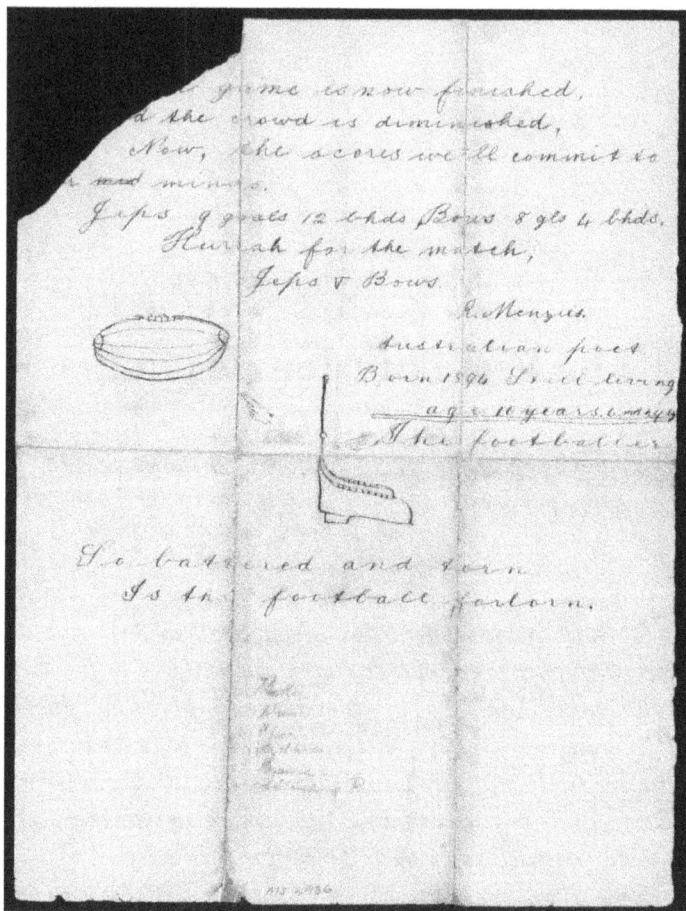

The page on which a 10 year old Robert Menzies wrote his earliest surviving poem 'Jeps vs Bows', complete with sketches of a football and boots.

Source: National Library of Australia: http://nla.gov.au/nla.obj-2892252187

Jeps vs Bows

Written at the age of 10, this poem refers to a spectacular local football match Robert Menzies attended in his youth. With 'Jeps' referring to 'Jeparit' and 'Bows' referring to 'Rainbow' the nearby town, and no doubt great rival of the 'Jeps'.

(1) Roy Street is in a bustle.
For that street, - made by Russel
Is crowded with people
All anxious to see the great match
Jeps vs Bows

(2) Great Boys, and small boys,
And men in galore;
Not to mention the ladies,
And the girls to be sure.
All to see the great match,
Jeps vs Bows.

(3) The match is now started,
And the men have soon darted
Away with the ball to the North,
From which place it is punted by Alf Garwith
And this in the match,
Jeps vs. Bows.

(4) The game is soon hot
And how to get cool puzzles the mind,
For the seasons are as follows: -
Bows 6 goals, Jeps 6 goals 1 behind.
But it all comes in a match like,
Jeps vs Bows.

(5) The game is now finished
And the crowd is diminished,
Now, the scores will commit to minds.
Jeps 9 goals 2 behinds,
Bows 8 goals 4 behinds.
Hurrah for the match;
Jeps vs Bows

R. Menzies
Australian poet
Born 1894 Still living
Age 10 years. 6 March
The footballers
So battered and torn
Is the football forlorn.

Robert Menzies, 'Jeps vs Bows', Robert Menzies Papers, MS 4936, Series 10, Box 355, Folders 3-4, National Library of Australia, Canberra

Animi Patrum

This poem featured in the 1912 edition of The Wesley College Chronicle, when Robert Menzies was awarded the Mr. C. L. Andrews' Prize for poetry.

Through the long years the minstrels have been singing
       The praise of martial heroes in their songs,
The clash of battle and the deadliest carnage,
       The rude tempestuous righting of men's wrongs.
The "thin red line" that fought its way to glory,
       The Light Brigade that rode through shot and shell;
The stubborn squares that beat back every onset:
       'Tis of these heroes that their stories tell!

And well, indeed, that round their noble actions
       The glamour of tradition should be thrown;
Well for the might and glory of our Empire
       That their surpassing deeds should stir our own!
But not alone within the battle's maelstrom
       Have heroes marked their deeds in scrolls of fame,
For peace shrouds acts of sacrificing courage,
       And many a hero dies, without a name!

Long years ago, when o'er our sunny landscape
       The black man held his old nomadic sway,
The bearded pioneers of a new nation
       Set forth in the wilds to find a way.
One was the spirit that impelled the wand'rings
       Of Leichardt (in some unknown grave he's laid!),
Or that which left brave Burke and Wills to perish
       Beneath the drooping gumtrees' scanty shade.

Our days of searching and of quest are over,
      The horror and the shock of war unknown;
But we may mould our life and thought and action,
      And shape our nationhood, in peace alone!
Ours is the heritage of all that's noble,
      The sacrifice of years that have gone by;
The deeds our fathers did when they were mortal
      Shall guide our steps, like voices from the sky!

But whether in the din of some great combat,
      Or in the milder walks of civil life,
The spirit that our yesterdays bequeath us
      Shall watch our beings in their daily strife.
And may we show, to all the world, the presence
      Of that same courage that enriches men;
Forgetting self, we'd hear the commendation:
      'The heroes of the ages live again!'

Wesley College Melbourne, VIC. *Chronicle 1912, No_136 December*, **December 1912**

A tribute from Menzies to Billy Hughes

This verse was written about former Prime Minister Billy Hughes and was set to the tune of 'PC Forty-Nine' for the Student's Representative Council at the University of Melbourne.

When Billy went to England he was just a little chap
Who ruled the Labour caucus with his stern parental rap,
But for the other party, well, he didn't care a snap,
        Did little – Billy Hughes.
He left Australia far behind, he dared the raging main,
He groaned in agony of spirt and internal pain,
He thought – I'll never hear O'Malley's roosters crow again,
      Thought little – Billy Hughes
Little Billy Hughes
Went to England to expand his martial views,
He stepped ashore at London and he hailed a passing car,
He had his Sunday trousers on, and looked quite "lah-di-dah,"
He called on Mr. Asquith who cried "Hullo, there you are!
      Right welcome, Billy Hughes!"

So round about the country-side they went from day to day,
The people came in thousands to hear what they had to say,
Demosthenes and Percy Brunton wouldn't earn their pay
      Compared with – Billy Hughes.
They motored up to Glasgow in His Majesty's Own Ford,
The Scotchmen's mouths were opened all the time that Billy jawed,
Instead of "gud Scotch Whiskey," into them advice he poured,
      Did little – Billy Hughes.

Troy Bramston, *Robert Menzies, The Art of Politics* (2019) Scribe, p. 274

At Evening, by the Sea, A Song

I watched the sunset flush and fade,
   At Evening, by the sea!
When all the waves were touched with red,
And burnished clouds hung overhead,
   And peace was on the sea!

The pall of gloom and darkness dell,
   At Evening, by the sea!
I only heard the waves' slow sweep,
The breathing of the mighty deep,
   For peace was on the sea!

But then the watchmen of the sky,
   At Evening, by the sea!
Lit up the fiery orbs of night,
The stars flashed forth their silver light,
   Across the boundless sea!

Ah! thus, I thought it often is
   On life's uncharted sea-
One moment we are sad and worn,
The next, a newer hope is born,
   And *peace* is on the sea!

The Melbourne University Magazine, August 1913, Vol. 7, No. 2, p.50

"To Wordsworth"

Great Master, let us sit and learn of thee!
  Give us the sense of glory that was thine!
Show us the vision that we do not see.
  Of Nature's wonders, and of things divine!
We hear the thunder rattling through the skies
  We see the lightening's fitful fancies play;
We hear the wild waves and their echoing cries,
  And we are thrilled, yet know not what they say!

But, thou, blest Spirit, in the storm didst see
  A visionary power, strong and clear;
And, while the black heavens shrieked aloud with glee,
  A call to dedication thou didst hear!
The very grass to thee had voice to speak,
  The humblest flower had strength to move thy heart!
Then us, guide us ere our faith grow weak,
  Show us the sunset ere its hues depart!

The Melbourne University Magazine, August 1913, Vol. 7, No. 2, p. 57

March

As some lone minstrel, who, reluctantly,
　　Passing from grief to joy, turns not away
　　From those sad tunes which formed his doleful lay,
But lingers with a broken melody,
Ere yet his words may pour forth joyously –
　　So is this month of March a month not gay,
　　And yet not mournful, for the quivering day
Of drought is o'er, but winter's yet to be.

But cloud-flecked skies are here, and mutterings
　　Of the storm time to come; some showers to tell;
　　Of the great winter rains; with winds that beat
　　To herald in the time when mighty wings
　　Of tempest sweep the earth, and say farewell
　　To all the sadness of the summer heat.

The Melbourne University Magazine, May 1914, Vol. 8, No. 1, p. 14

"The Soul of Hope": A Reform Song

Out from the murk of the time that surrounds us,
    Out from the dull, carking cares of today,
Into the future with distant hopes gleaming,
    Glimpses of dreamland shall show us the way.
What though the world may laugh, pointing and jeering,
    What though mankind may smile wisely and long;
We, with the thought that is burning within us,
    Boldly will onward, our pathway a song!

Let the poor fools who delude them with folly,
    Say that our cry is but lost in the air,
    Let them assert, with their smug self-complacence,
    Failure alone waits the men who will dare!
There is behind us a spirit that prompts us,
    There is what tells us that dawn is ahead;
Time shall approve what we pace the lone path for,
    Spaces to come shall resound to our tread!

So we march ever, our gaze still before us,
    Catching a glimpse of the stars, it may be;
Dreaming the dream of a world that is better,
    Seeing the vision of men that are free,
Yearning to find the great day of our triumph,
    Lit with the glory of reaching our goal!
This is the prayer, and the life, and the hope of us,
    This is our blazing, unquenchable Soul!

The Melbourne University Magazine, May 1914, Vol. 8, No. 1, p. 22

Nocturne

When nights are dark, and through the trees a-sighing
   The Wind comes murm'ring at the window pane,
I catch the sound of echoing, far-off voices,
   And fancy weaves old scenes for me again.

Perchance my mind attunes itself to sorrow,
   And then it is I stand upon the shore,
And hear the plaintive music of the surges,
   And the great ocean's sadness in its roar.

But often, in the midnight's solemn stillness,
   Whispers the wind another song to me,
A song with words that tell of field and river,
   And the soft lilt of woodland melody.

Then, then it is, I seem to see the sunset,
   And the last golden kiss upon the trees,
And the tall reeds' sharp black against the glory,
   And the bright waters rippled by the breeze.

And then daylight fades and the night shadows,
   Creep o'er the darkened river like a pall;
The phantom shapes tell each their message to me -
   Some mystic spirtit holds me in its thrall.

So in the night, when all the trees are sighing,
   Murmurs the wind, and gently speaks to me,
And borne afar amid the great world's wonders,
   I feel its glamour and its mystery.

The Melbourne University Magazine, August 1914, Vol. 8, No. 2, p. 53-54

"Farewell Sonnet"

To the Members of the Melbourne University Rifles leaving for Europe with the Imperial Expeditionary Force. September, 1914.

"Farewell, brave hearts!" The simple words proclaim
  The passage of swift years, and the swift leap
  Of worlds to arms, and with no laggard's creep,
Your answer to the call. Oh, deathless name
Of glory shall be yours; your glowing fame
  Be one with those who saw the mighty sweep
  Of Trafalgar, and heard upon the deep
The guns boom out the sceptred Island's claim;

Heroes they were, and heroes too shall be
Ye who now leave an Alma Mater's home
To fight 'neath skies of strange emblazonry
Far, far beyond the rolling ocean's foam.
Poor are we left! Yet go, ye honoured brave,
To the right, the wronged, to triumph, and to Save!

The Melbourne University Magazine, November 1914, Vol. 8, No. 3, p. 94

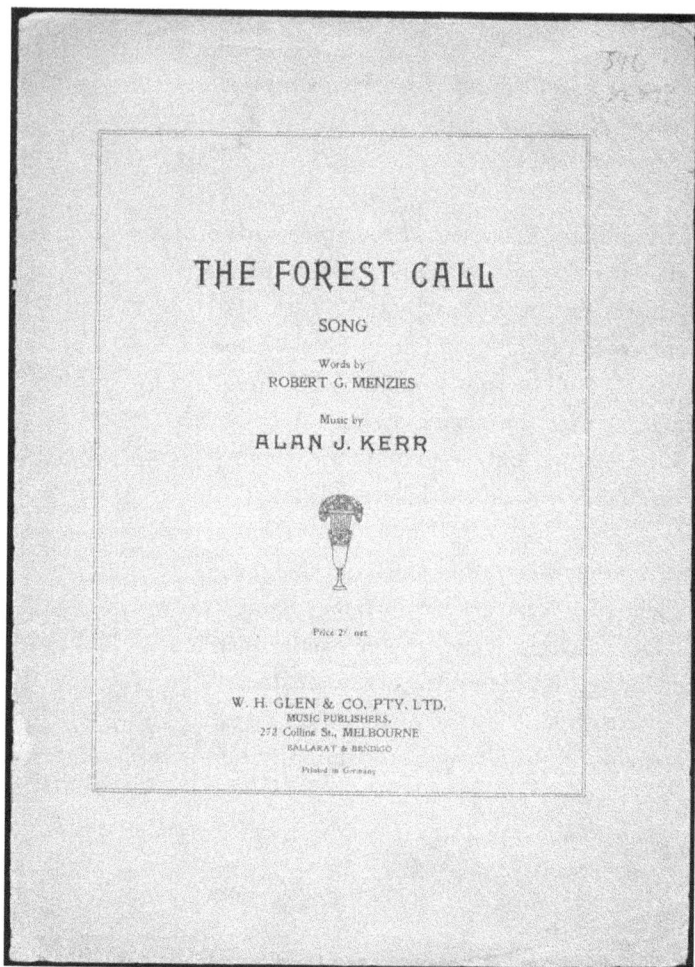

The published verse of 'The Forest Call' released in 1914. Menzies wrote the lyrics, while the music was composed by Alan J. Kerr – Menzies's contemporary at Wesley College who would be tragically killed in action at Pozieres on 27 July 1916. Reviews of the piece were mixed, with Melbourne's Table Talk calling it 'an attractive song, but of ordinary type, with fairly effective accompaniment'.

Source: Kerr, Alan J & Menzies, Robert. 1911, T*he forest call song,* W.H. Glen & Co, Melbourne: http://nla.gov.au/nla.obj-173117153

"The Forest Call": Song

Softly sway the branches,
Rustling in the breeze,
Whisp'ring notes of gladness,
Murm'rings of the trees.
Secret is their message, Words that none can tell;
Music sweet and mystic like some old-tie spell.

Over vale and mountain,
Where the fairies dream,
Floats the forest's message,
Over lake and stream;
Onwards to the city,
With its rush and roar;
Hearken!
Still it calls us,
Calls us ever more.

> **"The Forest Call": Song – words by Robert G. Menzies, Music by Alan J. Kerr. W.H Glen & Co. PTY.LTD, Music Publishers, 272 Collins St Melbourne. Printed in Germany.**

Minor Music

Sad is my muse, and melancholy strains
     of minor harmony
My fingers strike from the chords-refrains
     Of sad intensity.
I do not see the sunshine or the flowers,
     I do not feel the breeze,
For my soul's thrill is that of sad-sweet hours
     Like storm-tossed seas.

Ah! can it be that but so shortly past
     Is that fair summer time?
Our vision sprang to life, then faded fast
     Like echoes of a chime.
No more the idle joyousness of ease,
     Dreaming life's path along.
Shall charm, like gentle rustling of the trees,
     With whispered song.

Yet this new music has its beauty, too –
     The joy we feel in pain,
The star's bright splendour in the night's deep blue,
     The sun that shines through rain.
And it may be that the deep stream of woe
     That surges on its way
Will bring forth music nobler than we know
     Or sing today!

The Melbourne University Magazine, June 1915, Vol. 9, No. 1, p. 12

Sonnet (Written on a Twentieth Birthday)

So thou art twenty-twenty years gone by,
  And but a brief twelvemonth since last
      to thee
  We raised the birthday toast; what was
      to be
We knew not, and across the world's fair sky
We saw but Hope's bright blue. Who dared
      to sigh
  With dull foreboding? – but behold,
      men see
  Grim Mars in dreadful blood-stained
      majesty,
And weep to hear the death-gorged Eagle's cry!
So to unveil the future none may dare;
  Bold would be he who spoke of peace today,
When a full thousand bugles loudly blare
  And war-wolves roam abroad to hunt their prey.
Yet, though the clouds have come, to thee we raise
Another birthday toast – "To Happier Days!"

The Melbourne University Magazine, June 1915, Vol. 9, No. 1, p. 18

"To-----"

Oft have I purposed in my hours of thought
  To take my pen and write some lines to
     thee –
  Some snatch of song, some sylvan melody,
Some haunting strain that all my soul has
     sought.
Yet has my pen refused the grace unbought
  That charms the listening heart to ecstasy,
  Nor has the Heavenly Muse vouchsafed
     to me
The power to tell what joys the years have
     brought.
How oft we've seen it, lived among it all,
  Gazed like lorn spirits raptured at the
     view,
While the vague whisperings of a loftier call
  Were more to me, because full shared
     by you.
For this, the days that come, though dark
     as night,
Shall be for ever flushed with wondrous
     light.

The Melbourne University Magazine, August 1915, Vol. 9, No. 2, p. 49

"In Memoriam"

Lieut. J. R. Balfe.

Killed in Action, Gallipoli, July. 1915.

His was the call that came from far away –
 An Empire's message flashing o'er the sea –
The call to arms! The blood of chivalry
Pulsed quicker in his veins; he could not stay!
Let others wait; for him the glorious day
Of tyrants humbled and a world set free
Had dawned in clouds and thunder; with a glee
Born not of insensate madness for the fray,
But rather of a spirt noble, brave,
 And kindled by a heart that wept at wrong,
He went. The storms of battle round him rave
And screaming fury o'er him chants its song.
Sleep, gallant soul! Though gone thy living breath,
Thou liv'st for aye, for thou hast conquered death!

The Melbourne University Magazine, August 1915, Vol. 9, No. 2, p. 61

To A Mountain

Clothed in thy mantle of mist, O mountain
        unchanged and eternal,
  Calm are the days and serene on that brow
        where the clouds are asleep;
What though the tempest may gather, to garb
        thee in grandeur supernal-
  All undisturbed thou remainest, thy infinite
        vigil to keep!

Speaks the loud angel of death, with its
        trumpet-tongued summons sonorous;
  Terror has monarchy strange on the land
        and the sky and the sea;
Voices there are of destruction that blend
        in their hideous chorus,
  Winds bringing echoes of death, and the
        Whirlwinds of hatred to be!

Ah! but profound is thy rest as imperial rule
        thou art keeping,
  Laden with secret and song from the chaos
        of worlds long ago,
Bearing, deep down in thy dells and thy
        ravines with waterfalls leaping,
  Passionless strength in thy soul, but a
        slumbering fury below.

Temple of gods and of power, a citadel grand,
        yet a gladness
  Flushes with gold on thy rocks as the day
        lingers out to a close;
Glowing with russet and red through the mists
        that would hide thee in sadness,
  Bidding farewell to the glory and gleam of
        the sun as it goes.

The Melbourne University Magazine, October 1915, Volume 9, No. 3, p. 101

August

Winter, yet dawning Spring; the wet green world
    Lingers awhile to hear the fluttered wings
Of storm throughout the skies; the clouds unfurled
    In grand confusion, and the mutterings
Of tempest, where in awful vortex whirled
    The aery phantoms tell of mighty things
(Till fair September, with her flowers impearled,
    Enters with tripping feet and voice that sings)
The clamant messengers of winter are!
    Yet, see, the gloom has passed; the sky's fresh blue
Looks on a world that smiles and nods afar
    In the warm sun; the sparkling valleys woo
Their guardian hills with coronets of light,
    And all creation dances at the sight!

-R. G. M

The Melbourne University Magazine, October 1915, Volume 9, No. 3, p. 106

"Frater Ave Atque Vale" (Catullus)

Hail and farewell, my brother – aye, farewell!
   Darkness has come, to touch me on the cheek
And whisper shuddering fears, and murm'ring tell
   The anguished fancies that I dare not speak.

War – did it seem an awful thing to me?
   Did its dread music strike upon my soul?
Or was it but the thundering sea,
   With a majestic cadence in its roll?

Now, let the world pass by! For me has come
   Always a song, insistent in my ears-
Bugles of Death, and wild barbaric drum,
   Fierce shout of conflict---- broken-hearted tears!

Praise whoso list the pageantry of war:
   Hollow its triumphs when a nation weeps;
Faded its laurels if, for evermore,
   Sorrow, enthroned, a sad dominion keeps!

Yet, let the word be Hail, and not Farewell!
   Let the bright sunlight pierce the cumbering cloud
That dulls the vision, like some witch's spell
   Drooping the head that else were high and proud!

Proud with the ancient pride of blood and race,
   And duty done, and valour for the right:
So have you gone, God's glory on your face,
   And in your heart, calm courage for the fight.

The Melbourne University Magazine, May 1916, Vol. 10, No. 1, p. 15

From the French

When springtime smiled upon a world new-blown,
    I got for thee the flowers of May so fair,
And with their blooms for thee I wove a crown
    To gild the golden glory of thy hair.

Now with its tears the autumn sad has come,
    And on thy grave I place the flowers apart;
For the last time in anguish fierce but dumb
    I crown the golden vision of my heart!

The Melbourne University Magazine, October 1916, Vol. 10, No. 3, p. 84

Poetic Reflections of Menzies

While one could easily draw attention to his grand book collection of poetry, or his ability to recite Shakespeare at the drop of the hat for his entire life, Menzies love of poetry is perhaps most obvious in his early reflections on nature during his student years at the University of Melbourne.

"Confessio Somniantis"

I dreamed! And I stood in a dark land, a barren wilderness. Above me were rocky caverns, above me towered the bleak mountains. A land of death! Awful were the winds that wailed and shrieked, now sobbing as with a sad remembrance, now lifting a despairing voice in angered bitterness. A land of death; but I was not alone. Past me, with silent tread, there went a procession, white-clad, ghastly in the uncertain light. With eyes downcast they marched, and in their sunken cheeks, their dull stare, I saw no sign of hope. I turned – a figure stood beside me, pale, unearthly, hopeless. He read the question in my eyes – What men are these? What land is this? And like a dying echo his answer fell upon my startled ears: "This is the land of the Past; and these shuffling forms – these are the Ghosts of Ambitions Unrealised!" . . . I woke to find about me a workday world; the roar of life was in my ears; the call of action, loud, incessant, appealing. And putting my dream aside, I went forth. All day long I watched the evermoving tide of humanity, and listened for its still, sad music; and I thought that here at least all was activity, and the dreamer had no place! But looking again, I beheld a new wonder; for in the eyes of all I read Purpose; and understanding came to me, and I saw that these men had their dreams; that I also had my dreams; and for these we lived and died; their hold was strong upon us, and we strove and jostled on, treading the lonely spots of earth, confused in the mists and vapours that clogged our vision, but with the dream ever before us, beckoning us on, calling us with a call that would not be refused!

Again I dreamed! I stood I knew not where; for the land was dim to my sight, and whether the silence which enfolded me was that of the desert, or whether the land was rich, I could not tell. Far off in the East the streaks of dawn proclaimed the coming day, and turning to behold it I saw the figure of him who stood beside me. Gone was his look of despair; in the depths of his eyes there slumbered a great expectancy. "Tell me," I cried, "what is this land? What lies beyond these shades? What shall the day reveal?" And the man spoke. "The day shall brighten in the East; little by little shall this land unfold its secrets to your eyes, and, seeing, you shall understand, and shall be moved, and shall sleep again; for this is the land of the Future, the dwelling-place of Ambitions to Come!"

The Melbourne University Magazine, November 1913, Vol. 7, No. 3, p. 152

"The Blue Upon the Hills"

It was on a hillside that we had halted, and the earth lay before us-a panorama of green fields, and a ribbon of deeper green stretching across it, where ran a river. And, in the distance, the eternal hills, clothed with all their splendour of blue.

There was pleasure in all. Was it not Hazlitt who said that on certain lone heaths he could laugh, and run, and leap, and sing for joy? The same spirit was with us, and, though it was not ours to laugh aloud, ours was that cheerful glow at the heart that spells content, and that delicious wonderment which comes of lying upon the green sward and breathing the pure air of the countryside.

To the poor tired city dweller, wearied with the fret of life, the country has an appeal unique in its insistency, and so we found it.

> **The earth an ever common sight**
> > **To us did seem**
> **Apparelled in celestial light,**
> > **The glory and freshness of a dream.**

And then there was the river! Who shall describe it, with its fringe of giant gums, the sentinels as it were, guarding the mysteries within. For to me a mystery ever clings about a river; the relic, perchance, of a childish idea that somewhere in the spray of a waterfall dwelt the fairies. And today, as I look upon such a river, I am tempted to ask, Is it not so? This mist, is it not a vast moving phantom? Deep in that water, where lie reflected the everlasting stars, is there not the land of Oberon and his subjects? The mystery of it all takes hold of one, and shuddering he turns, half expecting to see before him a fairy ring, with quaint pigmies dancing round it.

Touch, for there is a spirit in the woods!

But to me the hills were as a thing apart. A wondrous blue lay for ever upon them. Of mornings, as the sun's rays topped the horizon, there were the hills, deeply amethyst; and as the day brightened their amethyst turned to blue. Day after day they lay thus, sleeping an eternal sleep. Nothing could surpass their magnificence. Silent, unchangeable, their indescribable blue left the soul charged with inarticulate emotion. Even so must Bunyan have caught the vision of his Delectable Mountains, with all their far-flung majesty.

And so, methinks, it must ever be. We bask upon the plains of life; we catch an occasional glimpse of its mysteries; and at times its awe leaves us trembling as a frightened bird. But, when blackest days shall come upon me, and I am like to be swallowed up in the storm and reverberation of the struggles of the world it is my fancy that for a moment the clouds will break, and after I shall see blue upon the hills, as I saw it then, and Hope shall return to me.

The Melbourne University Magazine, May 1914, Vol. 8, No. 1, p. 11

An Autumn Reverie

I love these sunny days of March and April, with their fleecy clouds riding high at noon in the pure blue sky, and, at evening, the long deep shadows lying across the hills.

It rained last night, and blew a little, but to-day is calm and beautiful. Near by there is the rioting colour of a clump of dahlias; in the far distance the hazy outlines of a mountain range; and, between, the plain undulates in sunlight and shadow.

Autumn, for me, possesses a charm above all other seasons of the year. It is the pleasant halting place in the journey from summer to winter – a season of sudden gusts and long silences that wrap the earth in peaceful slumber and still the tumults of the soul. Its old-world symbolism of death, of "falling leaf and fading tree," has here lost its potency. The earth is still green, not with the bursting freshness of the spring, but with the darker foliage of a matured growth; and, in those places where the elm or the plane tree have found a home, the yellow and brown of their departing glories serve but to lend a variety to the patterns of the great design.

There is in the air the subtle incense of dreaming and repose; sprawled upon some grassy bank, your hand shading your eyes, and the soothing sun bathing your every limb with luxurious ease, you drift unconsciously, and as gently as one of those clouds which are above you, into another world. There is a bird twittering somewhere, and a cricket has set up his lullaby of minor clattering, but their melody is purged of discord. Every sound sinks to a low monotone that seems far off. A faint breath of wind steals towards you, the grass bending as it comes, and you feel its dainty caress upon your cheek.

The world has become a pleasant place-of "mists and mellow fruitfulness," of dream-blue mountains, of wondrous sunny slopes, of cool valleys, where some stream murmurs for ever on its way, and the slightest sound is echoed back by countless thousands of invisible forest dwellers.

And so you slumber on, for it is autumn. Winter is coming; winter with its rain on the face and the sharp tingle of the blood in the veins; cheery warmth within, and, outside, the weird and fretted tapestries of the Frost King; season of life and vigor. But for me, autumn of dreams, and kindly skies; and, for my thoughts, the memories of things half sad, half sweet; of joys no longer turgid, of sorrows which have become (so amiable is the hand of Time) half pleasant in the recollection.

The Melbourne University Magazine, May 1916, Vol. 10, No. 1, p. 16

A Mountain Fancy

It is morning, and there is a mist over all the earth; a mist that steals up over Macedon and wreathes itself sinuously among the trees – for all the world like white and ghostly banners floating out towards us. The breeze blows but faintly, and, as the cloudy mass drifts across, darkly, through its veiling curtain, we catch a glimpse of red roofs nestling among dark green pines; higher up, the pale moss green of the ferns; and, wherever the shades are deepest, the tall white trunks of the mountain gums, straight and clean-limbed, true sons of the hills. Far up there, on the very summit of the mount, just where a jagged array of pines cuts the air, the sky shows blue promise of the day to be. What a scene to ravish the soul! Shade after shade of exquisite green, blurred and softened by the mist, and, coming up behind, the springing freshness of the sunlit heavens!

In a few hours it will be all so commonplace; the glamour will vanish with the mists, maybe, and trees once more be trees, and ferns but poor bracken at the best.

Somebody told me the other day that it was vain to look to Nature for proof of the supernatural, for most things about us were so ordinary, and even the finest scene so readily resolvable into common elements of earth and plant and atmosphere. But I cannot think that he was right. We are all so anxious to "grow up," so impetuous to taste the fulness of life, with its ambitions too often unrealised and illusive, that we are inclined to put away our childish things. We learn to "think big," and yearn, perhaps too much, after a fanciful and bizarre originality. And so the child of Wordsworth's majestic Ode sees clearer than we do, in that to him all is wonderful, and even common things "apparelled in celestial light."

Flower in the crannied wall,
I pluck you out of the crannies,
I hold you here, root and all, in my hand,
Little flower – but if I could understand
What you are, root and all, and all in all,
I should know what God and man is.

So the mist blows over the mountain, and the sun adds its gold to the green – "the green and gold of forest sunshine"; overhead all is blue and peaceful, and below, on the plains of life, seemingly so far off the fretting multitudes go on their noisy way.

And yet, in my heart, I know that this is not commonplace, and can never be; the hills have reached forth their hands to me and their mystery has entered into my soul.

Last night, at midnight, we walked home across the mountain; walked in silence for the most part, with the light of the hurricane lamp casting fantastic and giant shadows on the trees as we passed; up and up through bracken and bush that whispered as we went, and tall trees that glimmered, weird and ghostly in the gloom. The light shone on the back of the man in front of me, and to my queer fancy he looked to be always on the point of stepping into a black abyss. The thousand voices borne of leaf and tree came to us in faint noises from right and left. At times I was conscious of a vague terror that shuddered through my very being. And so on, till at length we passed out into a level path that wound its way among tall pines – pines that always seem to tell of grief and longing, and with the immortal song of centuries upon their branches.

Far to the south, just where the faintly starlit sky faded into darkness, a long glow showed where Melbourne's thousands slept, and below us the lights of Macedon twinkled their invitation. We ascended no longer. Down we stumbled – down a long dark tunnel, as it seemed, slipping on rocks and fallen branches – past huge trunks green with moss and weathered by years of mountain storms. Ever and anon we stooped to pass under an overhanging tree fern, and found ourselves standing in a little sylvan arbour, roofed in from peering eyes and carpeted with fallen leaves. To our left there trickled a tiny mountain stream, which filled each little gully with its music. Long arms of undergrowth touched me as we passed, and unseen spirits came from the shadows to lay their hands of coolness on my brow.

I will never forget that walk across Macedon. As the lights of home shone suddenly bright among the trees, and well-known voices hailed our approach, I felt like one who awakens with a start, leaving behind him a world of dreams. Foolish it may be, and in a sense almost absurdly "concettist" in its imagination; yet my heart tells me that there, in the shade of fern and pine, the ghosts of Wordsworth and our own Kendall walked with me, and my eye saw the pages of the immortal Book –

> **With holy leaves of rock, and flower, and tree,**
> **And moss, and shining runnel.**

And if that be my fancy, all things have become glory to me, and nothing shall deprive me of the glamour and wonder of the world.

The Melbourne University Magazine, August 1916, Vol. 10, No. 2, p. 58-59

Night Skies

It is fine and clear to-night, and the stars are out. The houses slumber in deep shadow, and the faint murmur of the river comes to me among the trees. A few steps, and I might stand on its bank, and, so standing, see above me the wonders of the "gem-studded night," at my feet the trembling reflection of the glories of the sky.

But I do not stir; just a glimpse can I get of the stream, winding its silver way amid the gloom, and I am satisfied. There is the smell of new-cut grass in the air, and the faintest of all faint winds comes up over the hill. Far to the left, long trails of light carry the eye on to the blazing illuminations of the city, and above, keeping their eternal watch over the world and its struggles, there are the stars.

Where there is darkness, there is mystery and enchantment. Pleasant indeed it was to feel the warm sun wrapping you as a garment; pleasant to look across the great gold-splashed spaces fading so quickly into the blue haze of the hills; but far pleasanter to gaze as I do now – when the sun no longer shows the red brick so stark and insistent, and when, beneath the pale lustre of the stars, the world has become a place, not of bustle and garish reality, but a place to dream over in passionless delight.

It was on such a night as this, no doubt, that Lorenzo bade his lovely Jessica sit and "see how the floor of heaven is thick inlaid with patines of bright gold" – a conception of the nature of the skies which has been real enough to many thousands of people in all ages. In these things we are all children. Astronomers, with their ponderous periods, and armed *cap-à-pie* with the fair chain-mail on scientific discovery, may give battle to our fancies, and, in the full light of the noonday sun, put them to flight. But the sun has long since gone to its rest; and there come stealing back to me, out of the cool night air, out of the whispering trees the century-old rippling of the river, those phantom creatures of the mind over whom the midday warrior had vaunted himself in victory. "Here in Faery," in very sooth; here may I recline in indolent ease, the while my mind, freed of its shackles, wanders up and up and from star to star, until it is lost in the infinite glories of worlds beyond worlds and wondrous heavens gleaming in silver and pure gold.

In this, methinks, I could be almost a Pagan. For when the stars are bright then does my spirit go out with infinite yearning to their calm majesty, and my ears forget all other sounds if haply they may catch some faint echo of their music. Two thousand years ago I might have come, and, bowing before these very stars, accorded to them the quaking homage of an old-world votary. I cannot do this now; but my fancy is prone to wander-

"Out on the far-gleaming stardust, that marks where the angels have trod"-

and, there wandering, comes a thought to me, that here, where men of old set up their shrines and worshipped the glittering symbols of mysteries that baffled and perplexed, is God indeed.

And, with the thought, lo! a cool wind that steals through tree and shadow, and touches me on the brow as if in benediction.

And with the touch there falls a sudden hush, and my spirit
bows down and worships in silence and alone.

**The Melbourne University Magazine, October 1916, Vol.
10, No. 3, p. 90-98**

A copy of the Sydney-based journal Nation. Published in May 1959, it boasted of shedding light on the artistic side of then Prime Minister Robert Menzies.

Source: National Library of Australia: http://nla.gov.au/nla.obj-2896356592

Menzies on Poetry

In his early years at the University of Melbourne, Robert Menzies not only wrote poetry for the Melbourne University Magazine, but had deep insights and literary criticism of his favourite poets. It is evident from the depth of his analysis going back to his time as a student that poetry was an important part of his life and something he forever cherished.

"De Natura"

It is a queer fate indeed by which even the modern University is inclined to look askance at him who aspires to dub himself poet, be he the veriest of scrawlers, or a genius born to hear the music of all the world. Take your student "poet"; he is considered queer, to put it mildly, and his sporadic outbursts, duly enshrined in the pages of a perhaps indulgent "University Magazine," are glanced at by the average reader, noted quickly by the length of the lines as poetry – (Oh, wonderful perception!) and so passed over, with too often a mental sneer at the expense of the one whose initials stand below. "Ah, well, he's a bit simple!" Voilà tout!

Is this right? Is it just and consistent that students who pride themselves on having at home an expensively bound copy of their Wordsworth or their Tennyson, should prove their utter hypocrisy and cant by ignoring cheaply the attempts, crude though they be, to express thoughts a little higher than the everyday?

I plead for poetry – poetry of the best sort. As an Australian I look forward to the day when Australian literature will take a very high place among the treasures of all time. This result can only be achieved by a cultivation of the best, and the careful fostering of all the buds of early promise, that abound in this springtime of our land. True, Australian poetry enjoys a certain vogue; but I am inclined to question the accuracy of the popular taste. There are many to whom Adam Lindsay Gordon's stockwhip melodies are well known, and "How We Beat the Favourite" may be glibly quoted; but how many are there who have walked with a greater far than Gordon?

How many have heard the thunder rumbling along the lines of Kendall, or seen with him the lightning play about the distant peaks? Kendall's ode "To a Mountain" I hold to be the most Wordsworthian production our local poetry exhibits, and Kendall our greatest poet; and why? Simply because he has trodden in solitude the wonderful places of our land; has trembled before the wild majesty of the hills; has watched with a poet's exaltation for "the filtered lights, and lutes of soft refrain, of many a mountain spring."

> Here is no reek of the stable!-
>> In thy deep, green, gracious glens
> The silver fountains sing for ever. Far
> Above dim ghosts of waters in the caves,
> The royal robe of morning on thy head
> Abides for ever! Evermore the wind
> Is thy august companion; and thy peers
> Are cloud, and thunder, and the face sublime
> Of the mid-heaven! On thy awful brow
> Is Deity; and in that voice of thine
> There is the great imperial utterance
> Of God for ever!"

We live in a stirring age, my masters, but at times it is good for us to be alone – alone with Nature, inscrutable as of yore, but telling wondrous tales to those who will but listen to her. It is good for the human soul, obsessed with petty cares, and smarting under its real or fancied troubles, that one should stand awhile and look out across the rolling ocean, the symbol of power and of eternity. At such times a vague sense of awe must come upon the dullest watcher; the music of the wind and wave is a harmony that cleanses and elevates.

We live in a world of work; a world often careworn, often sordid, often sad; but it is surely good that we should take time to search for another world – a world that need only be sought to be found; with the subtle appeal of its foaming torrent and its sweeping tide; and, through all, its inexpressible glory, and the wonder which weaves itself about it!

The Melbourne University Magazine, November 1914, Vol. 8, No. 3, p. 84

"A Century of Australian Song" (Part I)

[Further instalments of this article will appear in the next two issues of the M.U.M. -Editor.]

FOREWORD.

In this necessarily very brief critical review of the main work achieved by Australian poets during our short history, the claims, and, in some instances, the merits of many of the *minora sidera* in the library firmament have been subordinated to the main *motif* – the presentation in as brief compass as possible of the larger influences and the larger results. It has been inevitable, for example, that all reference to the verse of Barron Field should be omitted and that that gentlemen (who was no doubt a good enough lawyer, and wrote amazing if not excellent verse, as witness his lines "To a Kangaroo") should be deposed from his self-appointed place as the father of Australian poetry. Again, there is no more interesting personality in pre-Federation politics than Sir Henry Parkes, who was incidentally a maker of rhymes; but it and not as a rhymester that history will care most to think of him.

When this principle of reduction has been applied, it will be seen that our poetic output groups itself into three schools or periods. The first is the "pioneer" period, lived out among the influences of a new world, and new, strange ways of life. The literary parent remains England, and it is to England that the poet may still appeal, as to Caesar, for judgment. To this period belong Harpur, Horne, Gordon and Kendall.

In the second period the young colonies are "finding their feet" and, as it were, developing their personalities. It is a period of settling down, and has given us men like Brunton Stephens and Essex Evans.

The Third period is the modern, and its characteristics may be most tersely expressed if we identify it with "The Bulletin."

1. THE PIONEERS.

The present only is prosaic. Stray we ever so little into the past, we find the golden mist of romance gathering. Do we, in fancy, pierce the veil of the future? Here is fancy in very deed. He who studies the long struggle of the English Commons for freedom must always stand with spirit reverentially hushed before the spectacle of freemen gathering to moot beneath the spreading oaks of some Saxon village. It is with a like reverence that the Australian of to-morrow will look upon the names of that little band of writers, "poor poets of fellows," who were the first to add the songs of man to the melancholy music of the bush.

Naturally, in these early days, the influence of the old world is still strong; for this Kendall has made his own beautiful apology –

So take these kindly, even though there be
   Some notes that unto other lyres belong,
   Stray echoes from the elder sons of song;
And think how from its neighbouring native sea
The pensive shell doth borrow melody.

This is particularly the case with Charles Harpur, who was born in New South Wales two years after Waterloo, and died in 1868. His verses are occasionally halting; he has an imperfectly sustained power of continuous expression; from time to time he is guilty of periphrasis which calls a rifle a "death charged tube." But, in spite of these things, he gives us glimpses of a very real descriptive power –

"And, as they supped, birds of new shape and plume
And wild strange voice came by; and up the steep
Between the climbing forest growths they saw
Perched on the bare abutments of the hills,
Where haply yet some lingering gleam fell through
The wallaroo look forth."

That is from the "Creek of the Four Graves," probably the best example of his descriptive art. Kendall saw in him a soul that loved with his own, and could write of him-

Strange words of wind, and rhymes of rain,
  And whispers from the inland fountains,
Are mingled, in his various strain,
  With leafy breaths of piny mountains,
But as the undercurrents sigh,
  Beneath the surface of a river,
The music of humanity,
  Dwells in his forest psalms for ever.

R. H. Horne, the author "Orion," a classical legend in blank verse, was not Australian born, and indeed lived only seventeen years of his life here; but his name will always be associated with the beginnings of Australian literature. Just as the immortal Doctor Johnson talked mightily to his circle and exercised authority over them, so did Horne, the friend of Dickens and Browning, play the dictator in the first coterie of Australian literary men. The bookshop of Henry Tolman Dwight, at the top of Bourke street, was the rendezvous, and here, among the physically cramping environs of musty, second-hand volumes, Horne talked to (and was no doubt talked to by) an audience which at that time – the early sixties – included a young man named Henry Clarence Kendall. This circle must be considered a remarkable one. The colonies could boast no leisured or avowedly literary class; Kendall found it in his heart to complain of "the lot austere that waits upon the man of letters here." In the settled communities of the old land, among the green lanes of England, fragrant with memories, and the stones of London streets resonant with the hurrying feet of centuries, verse may come as a fountain that wells up; the atmosphere is charged with tradition, and the richest of all heritages for the sensitive soul. But in the adventurous south, when man was only beginning his struggle with wild nature, when life was, perforce, lived strenuously, when the wilderness had much more in store of bitterness and defeat, poesy might well have folded her broken wings and been silent awhile.

It is thus by a new standard that we judge our first essentially Australian poets.

Adam Lindsay Gordon was an Englishman of birth and education, born in 1833, and his life ended in 1870, with a suicidal shot in the bush at Brighton. In the intervening years he had gone to Australia, had lived the hard life of a pastoral pioneer, had sat in Parliament, had established a reputation as a horse-dealer and steeple-chase rider, and had, finally, one day awakened to find the lines he had written to beguile idle moments – mere *obiter dicta* of his life – famous on the lips of his fellow colonials. Beyond doubt, he is the best-known of our Australian poets; beyond doubt also his poetry is undeserving of much of the praise that has been lavished upon it. He was popular, and still is popular, because there has been for his singing voice an especially listening ear. The minstrels of old time found ready audience for sagas of knight-errantry and battle; the joy of the open air and the wide plains has led the Australian naturally to the galloping beat and "horsey flavour" of Gordon's rhymes. They are of essence for recitation, and not for the study. "From the Wreck," as a poem, may be wretched enough; but, skilfully recited, it has a carrying power that is convincing. "The Sick Stockrider," undoubtedly his best "Australian" work, finds a quick appreciation among men whose horses have been their constant companions, and who detect their own home-spun philosophy of life in the well-known lines-

I've had my share of pastime, and I've done my share of toil,
**   And life is short – the longest life a span-**
I care not now to tarry for the coin or for the oil,
**   Or the wine that maketh glad the heart of man.**
For good undone and gifts misspent and resolutions vain.
**   'Tis somewhat late to trouble. This I know,**
I should live the same life over, if I had to live again;
**   And the chances are I go where most men go.**

Gordon, in a word, is not concerned with the music of language, or the exquisiteness of expression; he is concerned with words in action. In all he is genuine, for, as Marcus

Clarke has happily phrased it, "the poet has ridden his ride, as well as written it."

And yet through all Gordon's apparent *joie de vivre*, there is the every-present note of melancholy. The tears are never far from laughter; and Kendall, himself a great-hearted, pathetic figure, sees unerringly "the undersong which runs through all he writes." There is none of that wide, calm contentment of soul that can make the glorious but ill-fated Rupert Brooke sing easily of "hearts at peace under English heaven." There is hurry and disappointment, and the fretting of a proud spirit. There are some exquisite lyrics in "Ashtaroth"; there is real pathos in the lines written to his sister on his going to Australia in 1853, there is no inconsiderable power of lively narrative in "The Roll of the Kettledrum"; but the crudities of much of his verification and the narrowness of his vision must prohibit Adam Lindsay Gordon, dear as he is to the imagination of Australians, from taking his place among the great poets of our national infancy.

It is on the young man of Horne's literary circle that the glance of the Australian reader must rest most lovingly. We see Kendall as a sad, wistful dreamer; a dreamer who turned to the city as to a Mecca, and found there only disillusionment and sorrow. There were few to care much for the poor verses of the solicitor's clerk; his fellow citizens, if they noticed him at all, looked disdainfully upon one whose craving for drink proved often his master. And yet it was through this very conflict, this very purging of self in the fires of a lifetime of tribulation, that Kendall's spirit became touched to fine issues. We look with a peculiar tenderness and loving-kindness at the grey, gaunt man who, in the solitude and grandeur of the mountain forests, ended his days with soul attuned to the psalm of the "grave winds," and the "liturgy of singing waters."

Kendall is a priest of nature, but with no note of passionate triumph. The kindly reviewer in "The Athenaeum" of 1862, when the poet was but a boy of 20, found that "the spirit of nearly all the writings under our hand is dark and sorrowful," and that the peculiar mark of Kendall's genius even then was "a wild, dark, Müller- like power of landscape painting."

And this is the dominant note throughout. He who reads "Mooni" (written in "the shadow" of 1872) will find it; the plaintive cry of the man who has offended and feels all the bitterness of remorse -

Ah, the beauty of old ways!
Then the man who so resembled
Lords of light, unstained, unhumbled,
Touched the skirts of Christ, nor trembled
At the grand benignant gaze!
Now he shrinks before the splendid
Face of Deity offended,
All the loveliness is ended!
All the beauty of old ways.

In all this the critic will find much of imperfection. Kendall's vocabulary is limited, and repetition of a favoured phrase wearies; his alliteration is excessive; he often writes for mere writing's sake; his range at best is a narrow one. But after all, we have had no poet yet of orchestral fulness; we must listen eagerly and gratefully for the sweet note of the individual —

the "lutes of soft restrain." Kendall himself knows it -

No song is here
Of mighty compass, for my singing robes
I've worn in stolen moments.

It is to the "Songs from the Mountains" that we must turn if
we would have of the best that Kendall gives. His dedicatory
lines, "To a Mountain," really merit quotation in full.
Wordsworthian in the roll of their blank verse, they are also
Wordsworthian in their loftiness and their natural religion -

Thou my Bible art
With holy leaves of rock and flower, and tree,
And moss, and shining runnel; … In the psalm
Of thy grave winds, and in the liturgy
Of singing waters, lo! my soul has heard
The higher worship.

and later-

On Thy awful brow
Is Deity, and in that voice of Thine
There is the great imperial utterance
Of God for ever!

It was perhaps natural that one whose life held little of joy
and much indeed of acute suffering should sing rather of the
shadow than of the light. When he looks backward, it is to
the tune, "When lost Francesco sobbed her broken tale," or to
the legend of Hy-brasil with its closing note of yearning and
unattainment.

But beyond the halls of sunset, but within the wondrous West,
On the rose-red seas of evening, sails the Garden of the Blest.

Kendall is not always sorrowful, though it must be confessed that the moving pathos of "After Many Years" or "Outre Mer" is characteristic; poet like, his mind goes out to the song he cannot sing – vain gropings towards the impalpable world of imagination always just ready to flower into song. But he is at least always subdued. His "September in Australia" begins almost exultantly - "Grey Winter hath gone, like a wearisome guest." but in the end the poet's mind has found a truth that is to it a bitter truth; that the song of September may loiter and linger for ever, but that his own must die.

It is plainly impossible to judge this man by the standard of an Adam Lindsay Gordon; it is but seldom that we find in him "the beat and the beat" of the wild bush horses. And yet, occasionally, the gloom lifts. In his lines to Tennyson he has caught the very spirit of that poet.

And lastly, Locksley Hall, from whence did
    rise
A haunting song that blew, and breathed, and
    blew
With rare delights. 'Twas there I woke and
    knew
The sumptuous comfort left in drowsy eyes.

We may have our sigh of regret for Kendall's bitter strivings in a world of men which was to him a world of harshness and of failure, and in the end a world of tiredness of spirit; pity it is that it was not his to feel more of the bright glad sunshine of life. But for everyone to whom the rolling plains and pine-clad misty heights, the musical mountain streams and whispering leaves have something in them more than matter, to whom these things have some gleam of visionary life, some breathings of an immortal music, Kendall will always possess a charm and an appeal that spring from that elusive quality we call genius.

(To be continued.)

The Melbourne University Magazine, May 1918, Vol. 12, No. 1, p. 8-11

"A Century of Australian Song" (Part II)

During the past twenty-five years the whole character of Australian verse has been so deeply coloured by the immense influence of "The Bulletin," that it would be futile to consider the writers of that period in any save on group.

But three prominent names must be looked at first, for, though Brunton Stephens, Victor Daley and Essex Evans, from the point of view of mere chronology, come inside the "Bulletin" period, there is a distinct cleavage in manner and matter between their work and that of Paterson, Lawson, and their co-literateurs.

James Brunton Stephens (1835 – 1902) was an Englishman born, who came to Australia at the age of 31, and entered the hard-working ranks of the "civil scribery." The routine of clerkdom proved quite insufficient to prevent a fine and scholarly soul from expressing itself, and Australian literature is for that the richer. Stephens was a staunch advocate of Australian Federation; his two odes written in 1873 and 1883, foretelling the advent of a united Australia, are a fine expression of the vision animating the minds of those who saw clearly the pettiness and waste of the separate and contending States' systems. His expression is Tennysonian: -

"For even as, from sight concealed,
By never flush of dawn revealed,
Nor e'er illumed by golden noon,
Nor sunset streaked with crimson bar,
Nor silver-spanned by wake of moon,
Nor visited by any star,

Beneath these lands a river waits to bless,
(So men divine) our utmost wilderness."

His dream is realised as the new century dawns; he sees –

"Our sundering lines with love o'ergrown,
Our bounds the girdling seas alone."

To the student of the war-interpretation and growth of our Federal constitution, Stephens' statement may appear rather the expression of a pious wish than an actual realisation, but there can be no doubting the splendour of his ideal-an ideal that speaks to the Australia of to-day clearly and insistently: -

"the task to build,
Into the fabric of the world,
The substance of our hope fulfilled –
To work as those who greatly have divined.
The lordship of a continent assigned
As God's own gift for service of mankind."

As is perhaps not unnatural in one who came to Australia as a grown man, and lived his life in the heat of the cities, there is in Stephens an absence of that characteristically Australian atmosphere in which the bushmen of Paterson and Lawson move.

"Mute Discourse" breathes a strong but orthodox religious feeling. Altogether there is that in his work which makes it easy to understand how it is in the English critic, rather than the Australian reader, that he has found his most appreciative audience.

His humour, if one allows for a somewhat extravagant indulgence in punning, is excellent. Some of the phraseology of "To a Black Gin" is wonderfully pleasing: -

"Thy nose appeareth but a transverse section;
Thy mouth hath no particular direction –
A flabby-rimmed abyss of imperfection."

His punning, often good, is shown in the verse -

"Thy dress is somewhat scant for proper feeling,
As is thy flesh, too – scarce thy bones concealing;
Thy calves unquestionably want revealing."

From his piccaninny "all unabashed, unhaberdashed, unheeding," right down through his "Universally Respected," "A Brisbane Reverie," and "From an Upper Verandah," there is a strong vein of humour that well repays the reader seeking amusement for an idle hour. "Convict Once," however, is his greatest work; written with great ease and technical finish in the difficult hexameter, it is one of the few examples of a successful, long didactic poem written by an Australian. Though rich in beautiful lines, it is scarcely susceptible of quotation here.

Victor James Daley was also by birth a "foreigner." Born in Ireland in 1858, he came to Australia at the age of 20, and had twenty-seven years of a rambling literary life before his death in 1905. His private life has been compared by one reviewer to that of Locke's "Beloved Vagabond," and the comparison seems apt. His drinking songs are exceptionally good, and he has Paragst's gift of humour "which rainbows the tears of the world."

"I pity those who have to walk,
  In sober ways and sad,
And keep a guard upon their talk,
  Lest men should think them mad.
Or careless speech should show
The felon thought below."

The title to one of his books, "Wine and Roses," fairly sums up the character of his verse – the fair level of lyrical achievement, interspersed with the phrases of melancholy that must inevitably come upon the Bohemian dweller in great cities: -

"The Fates have neither ruth nor grace,
  For weak or strong, for low or high;
The dust of dead worlds blows through space –
  And dust, and less than dust, am I."

His "Love-Laurel" in memory of Kendall deserves quotation: -

"Down through the clay there comes no sound of these;
Down in the grave there is no sign of Summer,
Nor any knowledge of the soft-eyed Spring;
But death sits here, with outspread ebon wing,
Closing with dust the mouth of each newcomer,
To that mute land, where never sound of seas,
Is heard, and no birds sing."

Another Englishman, George Essex Evans, came to Australia in 1881 at the age of 18 years, and died as recently as 1910. His work is good, without being conspicuously excellent. His longer poems, like "Lorraine," are commonplace enough, his shorter lyrics like the "Australian Symphony," and "The Land of the Dawning," being his best-known work.

"**Dark rose her shores in the seas of amethyst,**
  By tropic breezes kissed;
A sunshine land in watery wastes forlorn,
  Her ranges gloating in the snow-white mist.
And gold of early morn.
The tides of Empire ebbed and flowed afar;
  The thrones of nations in the dust were hurled,
Silent she slept beneath the morning star,
  A virgin world."

Other of his poems, like "The Nation Builders," are written in the swingline line now so familiar to Australians through "The Star of Australasia," and its brothers in blood of this century.

Evans may also be considered from another point of view. He sees that the songs of Australia are not to be as the songs of other lands; he sees also, regrettable though it may be, the narrowness of the scope of Australian song – "its songs of bitterness and pain"; he cries out for the richer and fuller song that is adequate to a rich and varied land.

No reader can fail to be impressed by the number of writers of undoubted merit produced by Australia during its brief history. As a people we may justly claim to be vigorous and independent; the wisdom of legislators, so much decried in these days of super-criticism and arm-chair strategy, must be given due credit for the splendidly universal opportunities for education and self-advancement. And education has beyond question meant that more and more people have heard the music and seen the beauty of our great literary heritage; more and more people have tried their 'prentice hand at the making of verses which, ephemeral though they may be, are yet a fragment from their dream of human life – "poor things," perhaps, but their own.

Of course, in all this one is brought face to face with the fact that a clever rhyme and a daintily-turned lyric are not of themselves sufficient to constitute a great national literature; but in so far as we find them, and find them abundantly, we may with reason claim that we have that foundation upon which great things may yet be built.

Our taste may at times revolt at the too fluent jingling of words on words or at the imperfections of ballads too racy of the soil; but great rivers have their origins in tiny things, and the turgid, muddy mountain torrent should never cause us to forget the broad and shining stream below.

(To be continued.)

The Melbourne University Magazine, August 1918, Vol. 12, No. 2, p. 57-59

"A Century of Australian Song" (Part III)

III. – "The Bulletin."

During the last quarter of a century Australian literature has been so deeply influenced by the native raciness of the "Bulletin" that one may be forgiven for calling this period "the 'Bulletin' Era." During the closing decade of the nineteenth century the tide of Australian thought began to set strongly towards Federation, and, although this Federation was the result not so much of grave external danger as of reasoned argument, the "Bulletin" found itself the spokesman of a people rapidly becoming conscious of their new and independent nationality. Breezy, irreverent, startlingly direct, clever with the rather pathetic cleverness that comes of cynicism, this journal remains thoroughly Australian, and must be honoured as the foster-parent of most of our modern Australian poets. There is rarely an issue of the "Bulletin" in which the purity of motive of some public person is not recklessly rather ignorantly assailed; but there is also rarely an issue in which there does not appear some poem of distinct excellence. The thing is characteristic of us as a race; we are a queer mixture of soft, low speech and vociferous vituperation; a thing all tenderness and arrogance; perhaps, after all, just a nation coming into its strength.

Very few names from the rapidly growing list of our modern writers may be mentioned here. "Banjo" Patterson always seems to one the voice of the bushman *par excellence*; his "Man from Snowy River" shows him the ready Gordon-like rhymster of the galloping hoof, the swift horse, the swift rider; the very odour of the chase. But his eyes see farther than his; his "Clancy" has the eyes of the body and of the soul open to see.

> **And he sees the vision splendid of the sunlit**
> **plains extended,**
> **And at night the wondrous glory of the ever-**
> **lasting stars.**

Henry Lawson, the author of some unforgettable vignettes of real life (witness "Jimmy Woodser") and some stirring poems of prophetic colour like "The Star of Australasia," in which the poet sees truly enough "the wings of the tempest whirl the mists of our dawn away," is, or at least was until the advent of the "Sentimental Bloke," the most popular of our living poets, but one may be given leave to doubt if, after all, his is the kind of work that that the world will not willingly let die.

Of the great majority of our modern scribes very little can be said. Roderic Quinn, a regular contributor to the Bulletin has a sure and very gracious command of the lyric; Will Lawson's subjects are chiefly of the sea – his virile poems are full of the rhythmic throb of the engine room. Will H. Ogilvie, now resident in Scotland, bears yet in his mind the pictures of a sunny Australia, and is responsible for one of the most striking tributes yet paid to the men of Anzac. J. B. O'Hara, amidst all the humdrum and toil of a dominie's lot, has yet found time to weave romance about the "Happy Creeks" of his native State. John Sandes was for some years famous as "Oriel," of the "Argus," and faithfully performed the exacting duties that fall to the lot of the poet laureate of the "Passing Show." James Lister Cuthbertson, the author of "Barwon Ballads," was a sort of local Henry Newbolt, and will always find an appreciative audience amongst public school boys and any others to whom "the forward sweep, the backward leap, that speed the flying craft," make their insistent appeal.

Bernard O'Dowd, assistant Parliamentary draughtsman in Victoria, enjoys dreams assuredly not the offspring of statutes and rules and the stolid practicality of the judicial records. A strong and original thinker, Mr. O'Dowd has won praise from many discerning critics as our greatest living poet. Poet he undoubtedly is; but his expression is apt to lack that artistry and beauty of design which make for popularity. His most ambitious work is "The Bush," a long poem, rich in classical allusion, depicting the romance which shall grow up around the common things of to-day. As for Australia,

> **Love-lit, her chaos shall become creation,**
> **And, dewed with dream, her silence flower in song.**

Archibald Strong, Acting-Professor of English in the University of Melbourne, has displayed to advantage an extraordinarily cultured and well-stored mind in his translation of Theodore Banville, and his "Sonnets of the Empire." The latter, though their technical perfection occasionally stifles their vigour of feeling include some sonnets which can only be called magnificent.

C. J. Dennis, backed by a wonderfully organised publishing department, lept into an instant fame with his "Songs of a Sentimental Bloke." His subsequent works have probably done little to add to his reputation, but as a high priest of the language of the "dinkum" Australian, and as the accurate and sympathetic interpreter of the down-town "mooch of life," its deep, strong feeling rising above its rags and poverty and sordidness, his position is, for the present at least, assured. No review of Australian verse would be complete without some mention of the war poetry of Geoffrey Wall and Leon Gellert. The former, a Wesley College boy, met his death as a pilot in the Royal Flying Corps, and undoubtedly, as his old headmaster, Mr. L. A. Adamson, has observed, shared to a great degree the characteristics of that great genius, Rupert Brooke. Those who have any love for the literature of our old land will find much to inspire them in the all too brief songs of this young gallant who had perforce to lay aside his dream to keep his "rendezvous with death."

Leon Gellert's "Songs of a Campaign" are the work of a realist in art who fought in the Gallipoli Campaign, and has painted his canvas with the red pictures of war. He does not display any morbid pleasure in horror; but it is safe to say that nothing more vivid has been written by an Australian soldier.

If nothing has been said here of the work of Australian poetesses, of whom there have been at least ten of conspicuous merit during this century, it is probably only because the selfish vision of men has rested rather on the poets; because, in the growing vigour of a new land, our ears have sought not so much the songs of love and longing as the full-throated sagas of flood and field, the noise of the tumult and of the shouting.

The Melbourne University Magazine, October 1918, Vol. 12, No. 3, p. 105-107

The Shakespeare Tercentenary

The three-hundredth anniversary of the death of William Shakespeare finds the world still reading him, criticising him, speculating upon him. A Chicago court has even recently decided that Shakespeare was Bacon; and this decision, colossal and farcical stupidity though it may be, is not without its significance. It is at least proof that in everything save appreciation of his unrivalled genius, opinion on Shakespeare is almost as diverse as the critics are numerous.

Three hundred years have passed, and through their almost impenetrable mists we see but little of the physical man Shakespeare. A deer-stealing escapade or two on the lands of "lousy Lucy," something of a romantic love, and then a glimpse at Elizabethan stage; very little more is vouchsafed to us. But not the passage of three thousand years can dim the splendours of the great series of dramatic achievements which commence possibly with "Love's Labour Lost," and end in the serene mastery of the "Tempest," and a "Winter's Tale". These are to us the spiritual man Shakespeare; more than that, they are the spiritual England in which he dwelt, and the priceless treasure of the England of centuries to come.

For three hundred years Shakespeare has been scrutinised with the critic's infallible eye; his political views have been delved for in many stray corners; most of the professions and many of the trades have claimed him for their own. But he survives all critics, just as he baffles all description. To measure such a mountain by the literary foot-rules that are too often applied to him can be nothing else but grotesque;

possibly nobody would be more surprised than Shakespeare himself at some of the wonderful fabrics that have been built up on his obscurest sentences.

But of this we can be sure – that Shakespeare is the superbest genius of our literature – indefinable, constantly yielding fresh glories to him who seeks, speaking to all as if with a "gift of tongues," and yet doing all this with such consummate ease and sureness that we forget the poet in the man and pass without an effort from the drama of the players to the human episodes of the world about us.

We respect and cherish our Milton, but we read our Shakespeare. It is surely not too much to say that for one who has listened to the sonorous and majestic story of those whom the Almighty Power "Hurl'd headlong flaming from the ethereal sky," there are a dozen to whom Shakespeare is something more than a name. The reason seems to lie in this – that Shakespeare was above all things a man speaking to men. All-comprehensive though his imagination was, he did not lose himself in its fogs. The world of men was his study, and just as one, gazing from a window upon a crowded street, might, looking deep enough, read many a tragedy and many comedy in the sea of faces, so does our Shakespeare, going to and fro in his sixteenth century world, make record of what he finds.

One doubts whether there was ever genius less consciously strove to win himself a lasting fame in the world of letters. Conceivably the dramatist might, had the subject been suggested to him, have said with Lowell –

"It may be glorious to write
  Thoughts that shall glad the two or three
High souls, like those far stars that come in sight
  Once in a century.
But better far it is to speak
  One simple word, which now and then
Shall waken their free nature in the weak
  And friendless sons of men."

In short, Shakespeare wrote for the stage – for the many and not for the chosen few. And yet, to-day, the few and the many vie with each other in doing to honour to him who has expressed the thoughts of all.

Shakespeare is our great practical poet. Dowden has well expressed this characteristic in these words: -

"Dante – filled with keen political passion as he was – finds his subjects of highest imaginative interest not in the life of Florence, and Pisa, and Verona, but in circles of Hell, and the mount of Purgatory, and the rose of beautified spirits. Human love ceases to be adequate for the needs of his adult heart; the woman who was dearest to him ceases to be woman, and is sublimed into the supernatural wisdom of theology. . . . But, with his ever present sense of truth, his realisation of fact, especially of that great fact, a moral order of the universe, we cannot think of Shakespeare among the men of pleasure, scepticism, and irony. Neither can we picture to ourselves an ascetic Shakespeare, suppressing his desire of knowledge, transforming his hearty sense of natural enjoyment into curiosities of mystic joy, exhaling his strength . . . in tender lamentations over the vanity of human love and human grief."

Shakespeare may or may not merit the criticism levelled at him in Melbourne a few days ago, that "he was anti-democratic, and therefore a political menace." His politics may be what they may be, Liberal or Conservative, advanced or out-of-date; we in this century only know that in his pages we find passion and calmness, sorrow and joy, shadow and shine; a tune for our every mood; a great storehouse of sustenance for both mind and spirit, from which we may take and be satisfied.

The Melbourne University Magazine, May 1916, p. 26-28

Menzies's Occasional Verse

Sir Robert's daughter, Heather Henderson, affectionately and lovingly referred to his poetry as being "light-hearted" and emphasised the fun nature of them. They certainly showed another side of the serious 'Bob' that appeared in Parliament as Prime Minister for 18 years.

Mister Hughes gushing on the Empire

"On the Empire pour your gush,
Throw the Shop a platitude;
Shower on Mister Hughes some mush,
Strike a Loyal attitude."

The Melbourne University Magazine, 1917, Vol. 11, No. 2, p. 57

A short poem to Chifley

How d'ye do?
Is it true
That the wordy and raucous
Boys of the Caucus
At a word, or a sign,
Become noisy, benign,
Noisy as the French would have been if Napoleon
          had escaped from Elba,
Benign, as if they were listening to Nellie Melba?

**Troy Bramston, *Robert Menzies, The Art of Politics* (2019)
Scribe, p. 275**

A Christmas ditty for a granddaughter

On a yellow legal pad, Menzies wrote a ditty for a granddaughter about Christmas.

Over here, where the squirrels run around
Up in the trees, and down on the ground
Picking up food and hiding it away
For a very great feast on Christmas Day

**Troy Bramston, *Robert Menzies, The Art of Politics* (2019)
Scribe, p. 272**

Club fever (regarding Savage Club)

Robert Menzies keenly frequented the Savage Club in Melbourne. The famous anecdote runs that after being rejected from the Melbourne Club and thereafter becoming Prime Minister the Melbourne Club offered him a membership, but he refused.

You must come down to our Club again, to the place where the savages are,
   Where all we ask is a tall glass on the top of a gleaming bar,
And a good friend and a loud song, and a firm hand shaking,
   And a bob in and the last round when the grey dawn's breaking.

You must come down to our Club again, for another night like this,
A wild night and a wet night, that fills the heart with bliss;
For all we ask is a pewter pot, with the white froth blowing,
And a sweet smile on Percy's face – and the last train going.

You must come down to our Club again, to our Club with the vagrant life,
   Where the world stops at the front door and goes back home to his wife;
Where all we ask is a merry yarn from a laughing fellow rover,
   And an hour's sleep and fair head when the long night's over.

Robert Menzies, 'CLUB - FEVER' (with apologies to John Masefield). Robert Menzies Papers, MS 4936, Series 10, Box 355, Folders 3-4, Library of Australia, Canberra, 6th of August 1927

Heather's autograph book

To sign your name in a little girl's book
Is a pleasure The Fairies send;
For you turn the page, and wherever you look
You'll see the name of a friend!
But mine is the name of a friend as well,
For Heather's a friend to me.
Though I'm grown, and grey, you can never tell
How young I can manage to be.
It may seem funny, but still it's true -
We're as friendly as bricks and mortar;
For I am her father – ('How d'you do?') –
And she is my blue-eyed daughter!

**In daughter Heather's autograph book provided to
Biographer Troy Bramston.**

Shylock Scene

In 1955 the actress Katherine Hepburn had a fierce, but possibly affectionate interchange with Robert Menzies. She labelled him a "wicked man" after her perusal of his famous reinvention of a scene in the Merchant of Venice court (Act IV, scene I). Menzies had contempt for the final judgment and believed it would not be acceptable in the modern age, so he undertook the challenge (in very quick speed) to rewrite it.

Portia:

> The hair goes with the hide. The law doth say
> That, if by contract and by solemn vow
> I undertake to hand some matter o'er,
> I also undertake to hand that other thing
> Without which the first obligation fails.
> Thus, if I sell you land, I sell you grass
> Which winds its roots into the surface o' it.
> Or, if a leg of lamb the butcher sells
> The bone is in the bargain. Therefore, Shylock,
> Pay no attention to the fledgling lawyer
> Who tells you that, from poor Antonio,
> You may take flesh, but not its ebbing blood!

Shylock:

> O wise young judge; O excellent young man.

Portia:

> Nor is there any substance in the plea
> That Christian blood is different from yours.
> Indeed, the balance of the argument
> Sways down full well in your direction
> For Jewish flesh, if killed the Kosher way,
> May have no blood.

Shylock:

> O excellent young man,

Let me have judgment; for your legal lore
Hath moved me to impatience for my rights.

Portia:

Also, forget the thing you may have heard
From pupils of the poor Bellario
To the effect that if you cut away
Less than a pound of flesh from off this man
You'll lose your case; for any mother's son
Who comes into our courts to claim his due
May always, as his simple choice, take less
And cancel out the residue at will.

Shylock:

No clearer statement have I ever heard.
Come then, my judgment, and I'll hack his flesh.

Portia:

Softly! So far you're winning in a canter
But all the arguments are not yet said.
One point remains! Stand still, and hark to it.
If any contract made between two men
Provides the doing of an act of blood
Which leads, or may lead, to a liege's death
The law of England, which by God's good grace
My author, Shakespeare, makes apply in Venice,
Rejects, on grounds of public policy,
The whole arrangement; makes it null and void.
And, as you paid your dirty ducats over
Not by mistake of fact, but error of law,
You've lost your ducats. You now take a toss
And write them off to profit and to loss!

Story recounted in Troy Bramston, *Robert Menzies, The Art of Politics* (2019) Scribe, p. 281-282 and poem excerpt from 'When Mr Menzies rewrote Shylock Scene,' News Chronicle, 29th August, 1956.

All hail, the great CHIFLEY

This was an ode Sir Robert Menzies wrote and delivered at a dinner for journalists in 1946. Menzies creates a detailed image of the publishing industry and cultural climate of the time through comedic prose, and taunting narratives of his peers. For example, Menzies who had just been defeated by Chifley in the 1946 election, sarcastically states "All hail, the great Chifley".

All hail, the great CHIFLEY, whom six states obey
Who sometimes baccy takes and sometimes tea.
Fresh from the battle over Bretton Woods;
Fresh from the brawl on Rosie Kelly's goods;
Fresh from the Caucus and the A.L.P.;
Fresh from launching RIORDAN on the deep blue sea.

How are the boys, my placid Benedict?
Is it still true that JACK LANG has them tricked?
Is BERT behaving? Or are Paraguay
And Chile cooking up a break-away?
And wee JOCK DEDMAN, wi' his tailless shirt,
And cuffless troosers, trailing in the dirt?
Is it the truth that though wee Jock saw reason
To banish iced cakes from the Christmas season,
At Christmas now he gives rewards for failure
To luckless candidates from West Australia?

How's ARTHUR CALWELL? Is it tittle tattle
That before going to the daily battle
He kneels and prays for KEITH and FRANK and
WARWICK
(And even ME, alas! alas, poor Yorick!)
And says: "God bless the press, and grant me power,

To give out only fragrance, like a flower"?

And what of VICTOR JOHNSON? Does he still,
Given the right ingredients and goodwill,
Spout Lawson right across the Cabinet table
(While BERT sits drafting HODD'S daily cable)?

Then there's bold CYRIL, having such a spree
Drawing the teeth of brass hat Q. or G.,
Does he by habit stand beside his chair
Spittoon in hand, and forceps in the air,
And say: "Don't whimper, or I warn the BOARD,
I'll as old Chif. to bring back FRANKIE FORD!" ?

And so I toast THE MONSTROUS A.J.A.
Who owe their prestige and their noble pay
To ISAAC ISAACS and to MING, R.G.,
Whose names are reverenced in the Gallery!
I often sit below at Question time
And gaze aloft at the salubrious clime
Where dwell the journalists in their array,
Both blind and deaf to everything I say.
Look where the courteous KEARSLEY holds his pen,
Knowing his best work will be "scrubbed" again,
And that his script, those very fiery particles
Will be snuffed out again by "Special Articles",
While BURNS, like Lucifer, tossed out of favour,
Gives to the "Age" reports a sulphurous flavour,
So reminiscent of the fumes of war
Coming from some Peace Conference Chamber door,
That PILCHER, well advised by those who do know,
Dashed off at once and took a job with U N O.

A word just here about the A. B. C.
That body that has failed most dismally
To give full time to Cricket, but pretends
Jockeys and Starters, Scratchings, Dividends
And Puerile Programmes to sub-normal brats
Are more important things than cricket bats.
Still, for this crassness, nobody can blame
Their Canberra scout, (JACK COMMINS is the name).
His energies I trust He'll try to use
To help me beat LES HAYLEN to the news!

So Gentles all, our Legislators,
I give the Toast of OUR CO-OPERATORS.

To greet these wasps, these ever-present hornets
A roll of drums! A silver peal of cornets!
Blow on the sackbut and the violincello!
Lift up your voices with 'New England' bellow:
The A.J.A, our daily friends and foes!
Up goes the glass, and down the nectar flows!

Extract from O D E. 'All hail, The great CHIFLEY', 1946, found in Troy Bramston, *Robert Menzies, The Art of Politics* (2019) Scribe, p. 274-275

A short poem for H.V. 'Doc' Evatt

While he never won an election, of all the Leaders of Opposition who faced Menzies, 'Doc' Herbert Evatt was arguably the fiercest. Despite their deep competitive attitude dating back to their days at the Bar in the Engineer's Case in the High Court (where Menzies triumphed), it is fair to say that they respected each other's intelligence. Evatt was one of the key architects of the United Nations and Menzies had the humility to appreciate his nemesis. Menzies has highlighted at length the books given to him by Evatt.

"Wee modest crimson-tipped flower",
Why deprecate U.N.?
Give it a chance, it's bound to grow,
To cut its teeth and learn to crow,
Like grown-up, earthy men.

Troy Bramston, *Robert Menzies, The Art of Politics* (2019) Scribe, p. 275

A poem for Arthur Calwell

As a worker and brother from China, I love you,
But if you <u>will</u> live in Australia, I'll shove you.
I don't like your skin, or your speech, or your race,
But I freely concede you're all right, <u>in your place</u>.

Of course, my dear fellow, if given my choice,
To call you my <u>Brother</u> would make me rejoice,
With my dear colleague Bert, who attends the U.N. ,
I have given great thought to the rights of plain men;

We believe all are equal, all children Divine,
All plainly entitled to sun and to shine.
But the thing you must learn, in a country that's Labour,
Is that no man who's yellow can be a Good Neighbour.

If he's red or just pinkish, that's not really sinister,
He may even go on and become a paid minister.
But if Yellow his skin, well, I won't keep him long,
I'll send him to China by way of Hong Kong.

Troy Bramston, ***Robert Menzies, The Art of Politics*** **(2019)**
Scribe, p. 275-276

To the Clerks at the Table

This poem was written by Menzies for the Parliamentary Clerks. It was noteworthy enough to be published in The Times of London.

Two WISE OLD OWLS sat at the table:
Their wigs were grey, their gowns were sable;
They looked so sad, so melancholy,
As if depressed by HUMAN FOLLY,
Around them, carelessly displayed,
Were all their dreadful TOOLS of TRADE,
The STANDING ORDERS, VOTES and MOTIONS,
The STATUTES. MAY, and such like NOTIONS.
The GLASS, with sand so nearly piled,
The RULINGS (wrong), so neatly filed.
The BELLS, to call the MEMBERS in
To tread the paths of VERBAL SIN.
But WISE OLD OWLS must sometimes think!
Of what? Of WOMEN? FOOD? or DRINK?
Or are they, as they keep their places,
As really VACANT as their FACES?

Originally published in *The Times of London,* **30 January 1967. Found in Troy Bramston,** *Robert Menzies, The Art of Politics* **(2019) Scribe, p. 276-277**

The Clerk's riposte

If we look glum and vacant stare,
When wigged and seated 'neath the Chair,
Please do not think 'tis Nature's way,
It's rather service for our pay.
For if some thoughts we dare repeat,
We'd find ourselves out in the street.
So time moves on; we leave the MUSE
And lend our ears to Members' views,
We hear their claims, their wants, their quips,
We see their moves, and calls by Whips,
But we don't TALK – So who can label
The inner thoughts of the Clerks at the Table?

Originally published in *The Times of London*, 31 January 1967. Found in Troy Bramston, *Robert Menzies, The Art of Politics* (2019) Scribe, p. 277

A young Robert Menzies in barrister's attire.

Source: National Library of Australia: http://nla.gov.au/nla.obj-2908130770

A ditty for the clerk

The below is a fine ditty written for the sixth clerk of the House of Representatives, Frank Green. As usual, Menzies had a penchant for observing his colleague's behaviour.

When, in some lonely mountain stream,
A trout swims on, in silver dream,
And suddenly snaps an adventurous fly,
From off the mirror of the sky
He hopes that he will not be seen
By the watchful eye of Frankie Green.
When in the house the insults flow
And A. calls B. A so - and - so
And someone, with a terrific frown
Quotes the wrong S.O. upside down,
He hopes that he will not be seen
By the watchful eye of Frankie Green.

Troy Bramston, *Robert Menzies, The Art of Politics* (2019) Scribe, p. 277

'Archie's Lord's Prayer'

Liberal Politician Archie Cameron made a grand speech in Parliament, following the Lord's prayer, Menzies responded in verse with reference to his fierce and vitriolic mannerisms in Parliament.

"Now listen, <u>GOD</u>, to what I'm saying,
I fear you let your wits go straying!
To be quite frank, I sometimes feel
That I should not make soft appeal,
But issue <u>ORDERS</u> - in a voice
To make an R.S.M. rejoice!
So, <u>WAKE UP</u>, <u>GOD</u>, and make it snappy,
<u>MOVE TO IT</u>, it will make me happy,
<u>GET ALONG THERE</u> with our salvation,
And keep all members in their station!"

Troy Bramston, *Robert Menzies, The Art of Politics* (2019) Scribe, p. 278

Canberra

Robert Menzies seemed to have a love/hate relationship with Canberra. He wanted it to be prosperous and did his best to make it so, but was no doubt frustrated by the lethargic attitude and lack of impetus from other members of parliament to make it a grand capital city.

Ah! Canberra, Ah! Canberra,
What holy peace and quiet there
From dusk to dawn the fountains play
With alcohol on Mugga Way.
Month after month new buildings rise
If not with speed, at least in price.
Year after year the city drowses
Lulled by the lack of shops and houses.
Cicada-like the insistent drone
of Civil Servants on the 'phone
Hums in the background, whilst the purrs
Of kettles, which stenographers
Tend like a sacred flame, combine
To make the perfect anodyne.
Peace, perfect peace? Alas, 'tis fake.
No Eden but conceal its snake.
It would be Paradise on earth
If Parliament could meet in Perth!

Troy Bramston, *Robert Menzies, The Art of Politics* (2019) Scribe, p. 278

For Frank Packer

This poem was written on the occasion of the launch of Sir Frank Packer's yacht named Dame Pattie which raced in the America's Cup on Packer's birthday.

Sixty years young, it's past belief
That your life's course has been so brief.
But as your seniors, we can say
'Good luck, young Frank, for many a day'
A lousy verse, an ill-tuned bell,
That wouldn't have a hope in hell
Of reaching (here let young Clyde laugh!)
The columns of *The Telegraph.*
You are, let's face it, fairly tough.
You can be smooth, you can be rough,
Yet year by year you've done me proud.
Within the limits truth allowed.
There have been times, as you'll remember,
When you've been tempted to dismember
That splendid man, the PMG,
And just behind him, even me
And sometimes, when it came to taxes,
You've sharped up your verbal axes,
And then have said, to make amends,
'I can't eviscerate my friends!'
Two friends now think of you with pleasure
And lay up, as a special treasure,
The knowledge that, through thick and thin,
You've done your best to help us win.

Troy Bramston, *Robert Menzies, The Art of Politics* (2019) Scribe, p. 279-280

What They Will Say

A satire from 1960 about what the Daily Telegraph would say about Menzies when he died.

Well, he's gone.
Do you remember him? He was prime minister.
Not without parts, but unsound on taxation   For some
    reason or other, he had a puritanical objection to
    tax evasion. Even by companies.
We stop short of saying that he was born on the wrong
    side of the blanket.   Local tradition forbids
    that we should take on so technical a point.
But he was born on the wrong side of the border.
Not his fault?   No.
Looking back on it all, we say he had his moments.
Indeed, come to think of it, he was, for at least half
    his time, a good bloke.
And that's something!
  Every Australian, imbued with the sporting (if not
    strictly amateur) tradition, will say to those who
    now have him in hand,
            GIVE HIM A GO.

**Troy Bramston, *Robert Menzies, The Art of Politics* (2019)
Scribe, p. 280**

Cricket at the Savoy

Robert Menzies did not shy away from discussing cricket at the Savoy Hotel in 1953.

This is a very solemn night my friends
Though it may cheer up yet, before it ends
Here at this miserable board there sit
Men without skills, or eagerness, or wit.

The gloomy Hassett sulking in his tent
Saying: 'That shot was not quite what I meant.'

The ancient Miller, too old now to bustle
Nursing his 'something, something, something muscle.'

Lindwall with versatility inhuman
Bowling his slows just faster than Fred Trueman.

Benaud the bold, Benaud the Giant Killer
Bowls like Doug Ring, but gestures like Keith Miller

The infant David took a rounded stone,
And smote Goliath through both skin and bone
With equal art, but much less lethal fun
Similar things are done by Davidson.

Some people study kangaroos or fish
The duck-billed platypus, or other birds
Some practise late cuts as their dearest wish
But Jim de Courey concentrates on words.

Bill Johnston, smiling darling of Society
Bowler of lengths and widths a fine variety
But Tallon always wished he could know
Whether Bill's going to bowl it fast or slow...

Troy Bramston, *Robert Menzies, The Art of Politics* **(2019)**
Scribe, p. 280-281

Why doesn't he go?

A short bit of verse from 1961, when the public questioned when Menzies would retire.

Poor old chap, why doesn't he go?
He's had his chips, as he ought to know.
He did quite well for eleven years,
But then he gave us sweat and tears,
And made us yearn for the good old days
When the socialists sang their hymn of praise
To the ration book and the tight control
Of all that a man had, except his soul.
Poor old chap, why doesn't he go?
And give us some pleasure to – don't you know?
One vote up, on the floor of the House,
Why doesn't the old boy show them some nous?
Why not make a spectacular bolt,
Taking with him Spooner and Holt,
Leaving the course quite clear and steady
For our friends Arthur, and Jim, and Eddie?

**Troy Bramston, *Robert Menzies, The Art of Politics* (2019)
Scribe, p. 282**

A speech to the Prime Minister's Ten

Sir Robert was renowned for his love of the Prime Minister's XI cricket matches. In an after dinner speech to the Prime Minister's XI and West Indian team, Menzies styled himself as 'Prhyme Minister' and spoke fervently about the famed Test bawler W.J. O'Reilly.

Who is this man with creaking bones,
      This ancient uttering oaths and groans,
    Bowling round-arms, and that most vilely?
Sir, 'tis the ghost of Bill O'Reilly.

The Wit of Robert Menzies, compiled by Ray Robinson Leslie Frewin: London 1966. p. 108

An affectionate ode for a quarrelsome cricketer

A poem written for famed cricketer, Sam Loxton, who was known for his short temper. Loxton would eventually become a member of the Victorian Legislative Assembly.

Look out for Sam, O gentle stumper,
  For Sam will bowl a fearful bumper,
And follow through with great displeasure
  And clock the batsman, for good measure.

**The Wit of Robert Menzies, compiled by Ray Robinson
Leslie Frewin: London 1966. p. 109**

To chairman Tommy Trinder

A poem delivered at the renowned Lord's Tavern lunch to mark the success of the 1956 Australian Cricket team.

Dear Tommy, Greetings to my team,
    Lord's Taverners and men of fame;
Oh, how I envy you the dream
    Of Spring and Worcester and the game.
So, the surge of joy ring out
    From Tavern bar and lofty steeple,
While Tommy Trinder pays the shout
    And says to all, 'You lucky people!'

The Wit of Robert Menzies, compiled by Ray Robinson, Leslie Frewin: London 1966. p. 109

The problem of Broadcasting Parliamentarians

To speak or not to speak – that is the question;
Whether 'twere better in the throat to suffer
The slings and pangs of unaccustomed silence
Or, to take courage from the glowing lights
That shine above friend Romans' gleaming face,
And, moved by passion for the people's votes,
Speak to their drowsy ears of this or that,
Or even that or this, or nought at all,
While wild debate pursues the galloping hare,
And Mr. Speaker dozes in his Chair.

Robert Menzies, 'Unnamed', Robert Menzies Papers, MS 4936, Series 10, Folder 9, National Library of Australia, Canberra. p. 106

FOR A.P.H. (A Greeting for Sir Alan Herbert upon arrival)

Over the years Sir Robert Menzies developed a very close relationship with Sir Alan Patrick Herbert, an Independent British Parliamentarian. Like Menzies, Alan was highly renowned for his wit. Upon Sir Alan's arrival to Parliament House in Canberra in 1950, Menzies was more than happy to give him a grand welcome.

When A.P. was a little boy,
His father's pride, his mother's joy,
He studied, at the grammar schools,
To speak according to the rules.

Such skill he showed, such application,
Such verbal art and voice resplendent,
That in "the Forum of the Nation"
He was an MP. (Independent).

As such, he stirred up lots of trouble,
And argued with both verve and force,
And finally achieved "the double" -
The sale of beer, and the sane divorce.

But all the time our friend A.P.
Was much attached to prosody.
As years went by, his hatred grew
Of all the clichés mankind knew.

He came to love a stone unturned,
A leafy avenue unexplored;
To "finalise" he never burned;
He never called a lawn "a sward."

He never said "I hope and trust"
   He never "ventured to affirm".
Even when moved by deep disgust
   He called no man "a pachyderm".

God bless, you, A.P.H., I say,
   For showing us the simple way,
For scowling at the convolution
   That makes a good bath "an ablution".

God bless you, A.P.H., we say
   For bringing back to hearth and rafter
The ancient glorious interplay
   Of English talk and English laughter.

Robert Menzies, 'Unnamed', Robert Menzies Papers, MS4936, Series 10, Folder 8, National Library of Australia, Canberra

A short jingle about Frank Sedgman and Mervyn Rose (Australia)

Composed as they played Vic Seixas and Ted Shroeder in the Davis Cup Challenge in 1951.

'Good greixas!' said Seixas.
'Nonsense,' said Frank,
'My second serve stank.'
But Rose killed the oeder
By wiping out Schroeder.

The Wit of Robert Menzies compiled by Ray Robinson
Leslie Frewin: London 1966. p. 112

A Scottish Wedding

Below is an excerpt from a letter sent to Robert Menzies's son, Ken Menzies. He details the idiosyncratic but jovial aspects of a typical Scottish wedding. The particular wedding referenced was for Eric Harrison's daughter, Joan, at St Stephen's Church in Sydney. Harrison was a leading political figure at the time, being the first deputy prime minister for the Liberal Party and later High Commissioner to the United Kingdom.

"Doonald Stirling Taylor, mon,
   Ye've gi'en me sic a joy
To stand up here and marry ye,
   A bright-eyed naval boy.

But hark ye now to my advice -
   Be pleasant to our Joan,
Eat up your parritch every day
   And never drink alone.

Pray for the war to end next year,
   And for the Leeberal Party,
Avoid conditioned air, and you
   Will grow up hale and hearty.

The scriptures tell us, Donald lad,
   That Christ drank tea with passion
Alas, He could not buy it, now
   That Keane's cut down the ration!

Take the wee lassie in your arrms
  And set your senses whirling
Thank God we killed the Methodists
  In bluidy fight at Stirling!

NOW, BACK TO BUSINESS, I DECLARE
  YOU MARRIED, WITHOUT BLUNDER,
AND THOSE WHOM COWIE'S MADE A PAIR
  LET NO MAN PUT ASUNDER"

Heather Henderson, *A Smile for my Parents* **(2013), Allen
& Unwin, p. 74**

To Katie McLure Smith

Hugh McClure Smith was the former editor of The Sydney Morning Herald *and enjoyed a robust relationship with Robert Menzies throughout his years as Prime Minister. Notwithstanding their differences on many matters of politics, Smith's daughter Katie asked Menzies if he could contribute to her autograph book, possibly in the way of a picture. He responded with the following:*

I am no artist; No! not I
I cannot draw, and do not try.
Under the editorial eye
I'd peak and pine and fade and die
If Hugh should in the book descry
Something that looked like 'printer's pie'.
And so, dear KATE, you should apply
To a more responsive sort of guy!

Menzies did in fact draw a portrait of his face and sign this poem. In response he was no doubt delighted to receive a letter of gratitude from Hugh:

Dear Bob,

How nice of you to find the time
To send my daughter that gay rhyme.
She will, I know, be quite enthralled
Though I am just a bit appalled
That you should think and write of me
As one so lost to charity
That what you call my editorial
Eye would simply be censorial

Were you to try to be pictorial.
Besides, how could I take the part
Of those who practice *Modern* Art,
And then deny to you possession
Of freedom in your self-expression,
However strange the form it took
In dignifying Katherine's book?
Yours ever,
    Hugh

Heather Henderson, *A Smile for my Parents* **(2013), p. 74-75**

Two books in the Robert Menzies Collection include a book-plate designed by James Stuart MacDonald. This plate predates the more common Lionel Lindsay book-plate.

Source: The Robert Menzies Collection, Melbourne.

Other Writings of R.G. Menzies

Australia at War: Broadcast Addresses and Statements by R.G. Menzies (1939)

A People's War: Speeches (1941)

Dark and Hurrying Days: Menzies' 1941 Diary (edited by A.W. Martin and Patsy Hardy, 1993)

The Forgotten People, and Other Studies in Democracy (1943, Republished in 2020 by Connor Court Publishing)

Speech is of Time: Selected Speeches and Writings (1958)

The Changing Commonwealth (1960)

Central Power in the Australian Commonwealth (1967)

Afternoon Light: Some Memoirs of Men and Events (1967)

The Measure of the Years (1970)

THE ROBERT MENZIES INSTITUTE at the University of Melbourne is a prime ministerial library and museum established to honour Australia's longest serving Prime Minister, Robert Menzies. The Robert Menzies Institute was established by the University of Melbourne and the Menzies Research Centre in April 2021. The Institute's mission is to advance the understanding of Australian history by promoting Robert Menzies's enduring contribution and vision for Australia as a country of freedom, opportunity, enterprise and individual dignity.

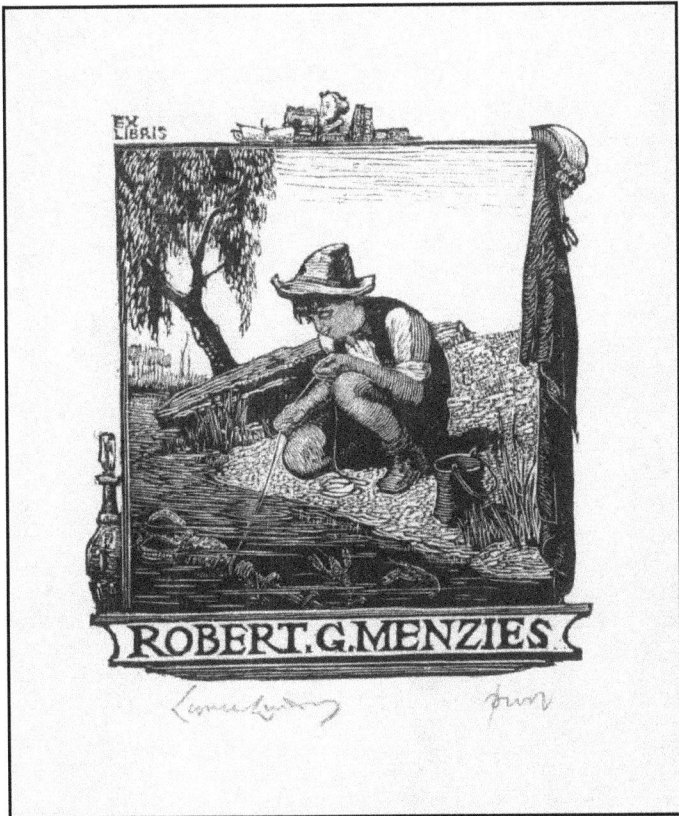

Bookplate for Robert G. Menzies, Lionel Lindsay

Source: Lindsay, Lionel. (1940). Bookplate for Robert G. Menzies, from http://nla.gov.au/nla.obj-141480820, used with permission.

www.ingramcontent.com/pod-product-compliance
Lightning Source LLC
Chambersburg PA
CBHW070335100426
42812CB00005B/1342